Like his previous devotional, *Real Jc*
has once again written an excellent
er's ongoing personal spiritual deve

He practices what he preaches and readers are encouraged to
follow his example in putting God first. This devotional manual de-
serves a wide circulation.

—Dr. John W. Lucas
Founder/President, MEA Worldwide

Will You Follow Him? is an inspirational read. John captures practical
applications from both familiar and not-so-familiar biblical texts that
will bless, challenge, and inspire the reader. His warm and reada-
ble writing style makes for insightful snippets of larger provocative
thoughts.

I heartily recommend this devotional to anyone wanting a
meaningful and impacting kickstart to their day.

—Eli Miller
Minister-at-large, life coach, and author of bestselling autobiography
Faith and Frontiers: My Journey Pursuing Destiny's Call

— 100 DAILY DEVOTIONALS —

WILL
YOU
FOLLOW
Him?

JOHN TROYER

WILL YOU FOLLOW HIM?
Copyright © 2024 by John Troyer

ISBN: 978-1-4866-2598-7
eBook ISBN: 978-1-4866-2599-4

Word Alive Press
119 De Baets Street Winnipeg, MB R2J 3R9
www.wordalivepress.ca

WORD ALIVE
—P R E S S—

Cataloguing in Publication information can be obtained from Library and
Archives Canada.

DEDICATION

THIS BOOK IS dedicated to the memory of my mother, Della Darleen (Oswald) Troyer. Everyone called her Darleen. She grew up in the small town of Beaver Crossing, Nebraska and graduated from high school there in 1946. She and Dad were married in 1947.

When I was three or four years old, she attended a George Brunk revival meeting and her life changed. I remember the atmosphere in our house changing as well.

She had eight children and we were all far from perfect, but she loved us all with the same love she had for Jesus. One day while dropping off some cream at the dairy, an old man used the name of Jesus as a swear word. I watched as Mom burst into tears, then respectfully went to the old man and asked him to please not disrespect the name of Jesus, her Saviour.

Many years later, while Mom was in the late stages of cancer, I struggled with an invitation to join a mission in northern British Colombia. We would be a long way from home and her daily visits with her only grandchild, who was eight months old, would become yearly visits. I was torn and couldn't make that painful decision, until her passion for loving and serving Jesus motivated me to action. It happened one evening when I stopped by to see her on my way home from work. She asked me what I had decided and I answered simply, "I don't know." She looked me in the eye and said, "I would rather have you halfway around the world serving the Lord than sitting here waiting for me to die."

We moved and began a whole new life a few weeks later. Just four months after we left, she moved as well and began a whole new life, eternally healed and pain-free in the presence of Jesus, her Lord.

The memory of her life still inspires us to love and obey the One who said, "Follow Me."

INTRODUCTION

THE HISTORIC REACTIONS to Jesus and His teachings weren't much different than the way people react to Him today.

Some had such strong hatred that they wanted Him destroyed.

A few chose the opposite extreme and abandoned everything, including their own lives, to follow Jesus as a disciple.

Many others came to Him because they believed He could resolve the desperate situations they faced. They received healing simply because they believed. Then they went their way, many of them never being heard from again.

Others came with questions about eternal things and were told, "You must be born again." That answer stimulated other questions, like "How?" The truth Jesus gave them is just as complete and life-changing for us today.

Will I come to Him just to get my physical needs filled and then go happily on my way? Will I be born again simply to satisfy my desire for eternal life, but use all my energy to try gaining security and satisfaction from this natural world?

There is a higher way and it also comes with conditions that must be met. It's one thing to relate to Jesus as my Saviour, but something totally different to relate to Him as my Master. When He calls, will I follow Him as a disciple?

Day One

I MUST SEE HIM

Philip saith unto him, Lord, show us the Father, and it sufficeth us.

Jesus saith unto him, Have I been so long time with you, and yet hast thou not known me, Philip? he that hath seen me hath seen the Father; and how sayest thou then, Show us the Father? (John 14:8–9, KJV)

SOMETIMES WE ARE like Philip, unable to see the thing we desire. When I shop for a specific item at a store, the distraction of so many similar items makes it hard for me to find the one I want. It's embarrassing then when a store employee, or my wife, points out that it's right in front of me.

I have never been praised for being in close proximity to what I wanted. Philip may have felt the same way when he expressed a desire to see the Father. Jesus didn't compliment him for having a good desire. He seemed amazed that Philip could be so close, for such a long time, and still not know Him.

If that happened to Philip, who was literally in the physical presence of Jesus, it can certainly happen to us today. We can be in the very presence and power of Jesus and not see Him for who He is. Miraculous changes can happen all around us without bringing any disruption to our lives. We continue on, rigidly unchanged, but feel secure in the routines of our religion as we successfully go through the motions of worship. This worship has value and purpose, so it should not be stopped, but it has limited influence when it's only based on facts and information about God.

The story of Job presents a perfect picture of this. He had a lot of knowledge about God, was respectful to people, had a very successful life, and felt pretty good about himself. His whole life changed, though, when his eyes became more dominant than his ears.

> I have heard of thee by the hearing of the ear: but now mine eye seeth thee. Wherefore I abhor myself, and repent in dust and ashes. (Job 42:5–6, KJV)

When my eyes turn inward, life is all about me. But when my eyes turn outward, life is all about Him. Then it becomes possible for me to be a disciple and follow Him.

I can believe on Him simply by hearing about Him. But I must see Him to follow as a disciple.

Day Two

THE POWERFUL EFFECT OF SEEING

But when he saw the multitudes, he was moved with compassion on them, because they fainted, and were scattered abroad, as sheep having no shepherd. Then saith he unto his disciples, The harvest truly is plenteous, but the labourers are few; pray ye therefore the Lord of the harvest, that he will send forth labourers into his harvest. (Matthew 9:36–38, KJV)

JESUS GAVE US a perfect example of what our lives could look like if we focus our eyes on God and nothing else.

In John 8:38, Jesus responded to some very religious people who got offended when He told them they could be free. He explained to them the very simple principle that He lived by: He stayed close enough to see His Father, which influenced everything He said and did.

Those who hated Him and wanted Him killed were being influenced by their father as well. The fact that they had a different father was proven when they wanted to kill Jesus.

We all respond to what we look at. Jesus could see the multitudes and have compassion on them because His eyes weren't focused on anything but His Father. The influence of His Father caused Him to be moved with compassion as He saw their condition. He never made it about Himself, even when He was miraculously healing people. He could simply tell them that their faith had made them whole.

While He was busy healing them, Jesus noticed something else: the multitudes. And the compassion in His heart moved Him to do something. That's what true compassion does. It drives us to action. He noticed how few labourers were available to work the harvest and spoke directly to His disciples—not to the crowds who believed in Him and came for healings, but to the disciples who followed Him. These are the ones who would follow and do as He did.

Let your closeness and view of Him influence everything you do today.

Day Three

CLOSE ENOUGH TO TOUCH

And whithersoever he entered, into villages, or cities, or country, they laid the sick in the streets, and besought him that they might touch if it were but the border of his garment: and as many as touched him were made whole. (Mark 6:56, KJV)

TOUCHING IS A simple act that produces powerful, long-lasting change. If the touch is improper or harsh, it will have a devastating impact. On the other hand, a clean touch motivated by a clean heart will change a person's life.

Every touch has a response. I was intrigued by how my children reacted just moments after being born; I simply touched the palm of their hands with my finger and they immediately closed their hands.

I wish I would always respond to the touch of God the same way. But it seems like the uncomfortable touch of difficulties distracts me from the gentle touch of God.

When Jesus travelled to different villages, cities, or countries, people lay on the streets to wait for Him to come by so they could touch Him. I have to wonder if any of them got uncomfortable lying on the hard street! I don't know what happened to all of them, but those who touched Him were healed. Then what? Was that the final act? What did life look like beyond the touch?

When we reach out to touch Him, it's often about improving ourselves. This isn't necessarily wrong, because we'll get to know Him better when we reach out to Him. It will greatly influence our decision to follow Him as a disciple.

Let every touch make me whole so I can be all He wants me to be and do all He wants me to do.

Day Four

THE INTRODUCTION OF A TRUE SERVANT

> Behold my servant, whom I uphold; mine elect, in whom my soul delighteth; I have put my spirit upon him: he shall bring forth judgment to the Gentiles. He shall not cry, nor lift up, nor cause his voice to be heard in the street. A bruised reed shall he not break, and the smoking flax shall he not quench: he shall bring forth judgment unto truth. He shall not fail nor be discouraged, till he have set judgment in the earth: and the isles shall wait for his law. (Isaiah 42:1–4, KJV)

THIS PROPHECY OF Jesus coming as a servant lends a perfect picture of what He would be like, and what He would do as He followed every movement of His Father. This was written hundreds of years before He was born, yet the prophecy proved itself to be true on every point.

If we're wise, we would pay careful attention to the first words God spoke when He introduced the coming Messiah: *"Behold my servant…"* From the beginning, God has wanted us to have more than a casual glance at this perfect servant. He wants us to have a good look, fasten our eyes on Him, and not look away. Nothing gives us a clearer picture of the actions of a true servant of God than following Jesus.

The original Hebrew word for servant is used more than eight hundred times in the Old Testament. It refers to a person who serves because of enslavement. This servant of God does nothing to promote his own desires, because he is overjoyed by fulfilling the desire of the One he serves.

How does this happen? What was it about Jesus that motivated His disciples to be servants of God? It looks like they were aware of four factors that dominated the relationship. They knew something David knew and wrote about in the Psalms:

> My soul shall be satisfied as with marrow and fatness; and my mouth shall praise thee with joyful lips: when I remember thee upon my bed, and meditate on thee in the night watches. Because thou hast been my help, therefore in the shadow of thy wings will I rejoice. My soul followeth hard after thee: thy right hand upholdeth me. (Psalm 63:5–8, KJV)

Isaiah prophesied that this servant who was to come would know what it was like to be held by the hand of God, chosen by Him, feel the delight of God toward Him, and discover the nature of God growing inside Him.

If all I have are religious rules, I will be a servant to them. Even though these rules can have a purpose, they can never produce the heart of a true servant, even when perfectly obeyed. Living as a true servant isn't difficult when you know the delightful pleasure of God toward you.

Day Five

THE RIGHT ATTITUDE

And John was clothed with camel's hair, and with
a girdle of a skin about his loins; and he did eat lo-
custs and wild honey; and preached, saying, There
cometh one mightier than I after me, the latchet of
whose shoes I am not worthy to stoop down and
unloose. (Mark 1:6–7, KJV)

GOD USED A humble, unattractive prophet in an out-of-the-way location to prepare the way for the Messiah, the greatest servant of all.
In all four gospels, it is written that as John preached, one of the first
things he told everyone was to watch for the One coming after him,
who would be greater than him. In fact, way greater than him.

The man God used then, and the ones He uses today, must have
similar characteristics if they are to preach a message of eternal value. Unfortunately, many preach the gospel with a focus on self rather
than on Someone greater, so the message is powerless.

My ability to faithfully serve God is directly related to seeing Him
as much greater than I am. It was prophesied that the Son of God,
coming as a servant, would have these marks.

He shall not cry, nor lift up, nor cause his voice to be
heard in the street. A bruised reed shall he not break,
and the smoking flax shall he not quench: he shall
bring forth judgment unto truth. (Isaiah 42:2–3, KJV)

This is a very simple statement defining the actions of a servant.
This true servant wouldn't be focused on loud declarations promoting Himself. He would be able to help the hurting rather than brush

them aside. The one who lifts himself up, making lots of noise to draw attention to himself, never has the time or energy to help those who are hurting.

John not only spoke about what Jesus would be like when He came; he showed what His character would be. His words were confirmed by his life.

Day Six

IT ALL STARTS IN A NEW KINGDOM

Now after that John was put in prison, Jesus came into Galilee, preaching the gospel of the kingdom of God, and saying, The time is fulfilled, and the kingdom of God is at hand: repent ye, and believe the gospel. (Mark 1:14–15, KJV)

I CAN ONLY imagine what it must have been like when Jesus openly declared the things that had been prophesied, and which people had looked forward to, for so many years. It may have been puzzling as people looked around and noticed that everything looked the same as ever. He clearly spoke the gospel, the good news, of the realm where God was absolute ruler.

The sad, downtrodden ones who looked for a redeemer were excited while the dominant rulers revolted at any change in rulership. They were in control and couldn't imagine being ruled by another. This is probably why His first instruction was to repent. In other words, "Think differently," something that's only possible when you believe the good news Jesus preached.

This was proven to me the night my heart was turned to God, when I believed and repented. My thinking changed. My thoughts were no longer centred on my own empty pursuits but on a kingdom ruled by a God who brings eternity into every area of life. If this change doesn't happen, we live our whole lives being driven by the empty demands of the temporary world; our greatest satisfactions are short-lived. True satisfaction comes when the thoughts that drive our actions are anchored in the eternal kingdom.

Before I can begin the life of a servant, my thinking must change as I believe the good news of an eternal kingdom.

FORSAKING OUR NETS

Now as he walked by the sea of Galilee, he saw Simon and Andrew his brother casting a net into the sea: for they were fishers. And Jesus said unto them, Come ye after me, and I will make you to become fishers of men. And straightway they forsook their nets, and followed him. (Mark 1:16–18, KJV)

IN THIS PASSAGE, we get a picture of the people being called to follow Jesus. What was the attraction? More details of this encounter are written in the first part of Luke 5. Simon and Andrew had watched and listened as He related to people, speaking to the crowds as He stood in their boat.

When Jesus was finished, He told Simon and Andrew to push the boat out to deeper water and let down their nets. It seemed like a useless idea, since they had fished all night and caught not one fish. But at the urging of Jesus, they pushed out and let down their nets.

Immediately their nets were so full that they started to break. They called out to their friends in another boat to come and help. They had so many fish that both boats began to sink.

After hearing Jesus speak, and watching how He lived, Simon had to conclude that Jesus was way too good for him. No way could they ever connect. They were too different.

But Jesus called him to follow and offered to make him a fisher of men. The inference was that Simon could capture the hearts of others and make them followers of Jesus, just as He had captured his heart.

Much of our time is spent working to meet the demands of our natural lives, unaware that we may be only moments from an encounter that calls us to leave it all behind and simply follow Him as faithful servants.

The call comes to the unworthy, who are amazed that an eternal God would call them to an intimate life of discipleship. Those who feel so unworthy leave behind everything they have and follow Him.

Day Eight

FORSAKING THE FAMILY BUSINESS

And when he had gone a little farther thence, he saw James the son of Zebedee, and John his brother, who also were in the ship mending their nets. And straightway he called them: and they left their father Zebedee in the ship with the hired servants, and went after him. (Mark 1:19–20, KJV)

GOOD FAMILY CONNECTIONS are so enjoyable. They become even more enjoyable when the family can spend the day working together.

James and John worked together with their father and a few hired men in their fishing business. Some days were probably successful while other days weren't.

This particular day in Mark 1 appears to have been a bad day when they ended up with nothing. It was the kind of day that set the stage for an encounter with eternity. They may have been in one of the boats that rushed in to help Simon and Andrew when their nets were overloaded with fish.

Just like that, a bad day became a very good day!

James and John were familiar with hard work, so all this extra work wasn't a problem. There would be a great reward.

But as they all worked together to bring in the fish, something else happened. The words and actions of Jesus stimulated their hunger for something greater. When they heard Him call them to follow, they immediately left their father, the boat, and everything they had previously enjoyed.

Do I know the compelling call of Jesus? When I hear it and follow Him, I will discover the thrill of being a disciple.

Day Nine

AM I READY?

Large crowds were traveling with Jesus. He turned
to them and said, "If people come to me and are
not ready to abandon their fathers, mothers, wives,
children, brothers, and sisters, as well as their own
lives, they cannot be my disciples. So those who do
not carry their crosses and follow me cannot be my
disciples." (Luke 14:25–27, GW)

JESUS DIDN'T GIVE people a lot of options when He called them to
follow Him. You would never be a disciple if you couldn't abandon
everything else in your life. It's a choice each of us have to make.

My encounter came in the summer of 1972. Life was good. I was
getting promotions at work, I drove a nice car, and I lived close to my
family. My wife and I were enjoying our first child.

One evening, a call came from a church in Vanderhoof, British
Colombia, asking us to move to a remote village in the north. It was
two hundred miles from the nearest road, had no telephone service,
and mail only came once a month. Somehow this fit an empty spot I
had been sensing in my life.

But I would have to leave a lot of valuables behind if I were to
follow this call.

As I went to bed that evening, I knew this was an important
moment in my life. Unable to sleep, I got up and walked over to the
church we attended. The door was unlocked, so I went inside and
sat on the steps leading down to the basement. I was impressed
with the need to let go of the things that were important to me.

At first, it wasn't hard. I could purposefully let go of my job. Then
I told God that He could take the nice car, too.

The struggle set in when He told me that I needed to let go of my little girl, who was only a few months old. It was hard, but finally I let go.

My process of letting go intensified when God showed me that I would even need to let go of my wife Betsy. I didn't see how God could put me in such a difficult place. Despite all my questions and fears, I let go of everything so I could follow Him.

I went back to bed and slept.

The next morning, I said goodbye to my wife and baby, wondering if I would ever see them again. I got in the car to drive to work and put on my seatbelt. I had never used a seatbelt, but I was worried I might get into an accident, since I had given everything to God. I didn't want to get hurt.

Instead of everything being taken from me, it was like a great gift from God. I honoured every gift God had ever given me by committing to follow Him with all my heart.

When we abandon everything to follow as a disciple, we lose nothing. We gain many blessings directly from God's hand.

Day Ten

COUNT THE COST

Or suppose a king is going to war against another king. He would first sit down and think things through. Can he and his 10,000 soldiers fight against a king with 20,000 soldiers? If he can't, he'll send ambassadors to ask for terms of peace while the other king is still far away. In the same way, none of you can be my disciples unless you give up everything. (Luke 14:31–33, GW)

DECISIONS THAT ARE made without thinking through the consequences are most often proven to be wrong. While it's true that we can never know all the eventual events that will happen around us, we need to at least be aware of the possibilities and decide accordingly. There are decisions that must be made. I cannot stop the progression of life by doing nothing. Refusing to make a decision is also a decision, and it often keeps me from growing into maturity.

Jesus once told a parable about a king who discovered that a rival king was in close proximity. There would be conflict. But the king wouldn't make a move until he had taken time to think things through, especially knowing that the other king had twice as many men in his army. Why would the other king want to go to war anyway? There had to be a reason. Did he feel threatened?

One thing was obvious: whenever there are two kings, two governments, eventually there will be conflict.

When the first king realized that the other king had the advantage, he made a very smart move. Although he knew he couldn't win, he didn't wait to be conquered. Instead he figured out what it would take to make peace.

Jesus was painting a picture of the kingdom of God. When we start off in life, most often we're unaware of any kingdom aside from our own. But if we are observant, we'll notice that another king is on his way to meet us, and he appears stronger than us.

Jesus wants us to be like the king with the fewest soldiers. He counted the cost. We are to realize that the King we face is much more powerful than us. Yes, we can fight and live as though we have all the answers for a perfect life. However, the more powerful King is on His way to meet us. Therefore, there is no peace.

Jesus clearly stated that we need to give it all up and stop the fighting. We won't win when we go up against the strongest. We are to give everything up to be His disciple.

Great joy and peace is ours when we give up everything to follow the conquering King.

Day Eleven

KNOW YOUR INTENTION

> For which of you, intending to build a tower, sitteth not down first, and counteth the cost, whether he have sufficient to finish it? Lest haply, after he hath laid the foundation, and is not able to finish it, all that behold it begin to mock him, saying, This man began to build, and was not able to finish. (Luke 14:28–30, KJV)

PEOPLE WHO HAD any interest in following Jesus as a disciple had to be aware of three important requirements.

The first requirement was for them to love everyone, including their own self, although it needed to be less than they loved Jesus. This can be difficult, because the people we love can become the dominant focus in our lives.

The second requirement was for them to count the cost of going to war compared to the cost of making peace.

The third requirement was for them not to give others a reason to mock them, which can seem almost insignificant. But the real warning was about committing to building something without having what it takes to complete the project.

While it is necessary for us to count the cost of following Jesus, we should also count the cost of not following Him. How much will it cost to go our own way? It's quick and cheap to lay down the foundation for a life of not following Him. Anyone can do that without having any idea of what the finished building will ultimately look like, because it's mostly delusional and based on a selfish lie that will never be satisfied. The project will never be finished.

On the other hand, one who commits to following Him without knowing the cost can be the subject of mockery. If you don't know the cost, how can you know whether you can pay it?

Jesus clearly wanted everyone to know the cost of following Him. His interest wasn't in attracting large crowds. He wanted people to successfully follow Him. The gospel Jesus preached was meant to attract long-time followers who would successfully finish what they had started.

In Acts 20:24, Paul stated his intentions to finish the course of his life with joy. There would be no room for anyone to mock him for not having enough to finish what he'd started.

What are your intentions? Count the cost and then pay it. Successful completion is much more rewarding than being mocked.

DENY MYSELF TO PROMOTE HIM

And he said to them all, If any man will come after me, let him deny himself, and take up his cross daily, and follow me. For whosoever will save his life shall lose it: but whosoever will lose his life for my sake, the same shall save it. For what is a man advantaged, if he gain the whole world, and lose himself, or be cast away? (Luke 9:23–25, KJV)

IF WE CHOOSE to follow Jesus, He will take us to live in a kingdom that operates completely differently from anything we've ever experienced. Since His kingdom is different than any other, the requirements to enter it are also different.

When I consider these simple requirements that start the process of following Jesus, I notice that He doesn't require me to prove my allegiance over an extended period of time. He doesn't seem interested in knowing how much faith I have. He doesn't require any proof that I've studied hard or passed exams. There is no requirement for others to recommend me. It also seems that the opinions of those who know me well have no value to Him.

The absence of all these requirements accentuates the simplicity of this lifelong commitment.

After my wife and I moved almost a thousand miles to a different town, I missed a lot of my friends. I wasn't getting the satisfaction of my previous job with longtime friends. I began to ask myself, "Why am I here?" I needed to know the answer because I felt no fulfillment with anything I was doing.

I pointed this question to God several times.

One day, it was as if Jesus Himself confronted me. I heard these words: "You are here for Me, and that's enough!" I stopped asking my questions and just made myself available to Him.

It's not about me, and it's not about us. Jesus simply stated that anyone who wants to follow Him had to deny themself so the second step can be taken.

At the heart of denying myself is the ability to contradict myself rather than promote myself. It doesn't take much time to discover that I easily contradict others, but I rarely contradict myself. This changes very quickly when I see Jesus, the Son of God, for who He really is.

> Let this mind be in you, which was also in Christ Jesus: who, being in the form of God, thought it not robbery to be equal with God: but made himself of no reputation, and took upon him the form of a servant, and was made in the likeness of men... (Philippians 2:5–7, KJV)

This is why God exalted Him and gave Him a name above all others. To know Him and what He has done for me compels me to contradict myself rather than Him.

Day Thirteen

THE CROSS

And he that taketh not his cross, and followeth after me, is not worthy of me. He that findeth his life shall lose it: and he that loseth his life for my sake shall find it. (Matthew 10:38–39, KJV)

THE MOST INTENSE teachings Jesus gave were directed to those who saw Him for who He was and wanted to be like Him. Many people saw what He did and wanted to do those great things because of the success and attention they could get for themselves.

There's a big difference between following Him because of who He is and following Him because of what He does. If what He does motivates me to follow Him, I'm keenly aware of how I will benefit from following Him. This actually disqualifies me from following, and I soon go my own way again.

But when the motivator is who He is, the benefit is His. My following won't be about me, but about Him. This doesn't detract from the truth that I have received so much from what He has done for me. But all of His actions toward me have been motivated because of who He is, not what I have done.

Jesus was talking to a large group of followers one day and made it really clear that it was impossible to follow Him unless they had a God-given perspective. Without this perspective, they would never have the ability to deny themselves.

This statement proved to be true.

The account of what happened right afterward is written in John 6. Many of His disciples left and went back to their former lives, almost as if nothing had ever happened to them. The original Greek word translated here as "many" is also translated as "great multitudes" in other passages.

This was not just a few unhappy people. Jesus followed up this account with a question for those who remained.

> From that time many of his disciples went back, and walked no more with him. Then said Jesus unto the twelve, Will ye also go away? Then Simon Peter answered him, Lord, to whom shall we go? thou hast the words of eternal life. And we believe and are sure that thou art that Christ, the Son of the living God. (John 6:66–69, KJV)

Peter got it right! He knew who Jesus was and appreciated that no one else was worthy of following. Later, Peter failed a few times, but he knew who Jesus was and always came back to follow Jesus again.

The better I know Him, the easier it is to follow Him all day and every day.

Day Fourteen

THERE IS EVIDENCE

If I do not the works of my Father, believe me not. But if I do, though ye believe not me, believe the works: that ye may know, and believe, that the Father is in me, and I in him. (John 10:37–38, KJV)

JESUS KNEW HIS Father very well. Not only did He know what His Father did, He also knew who His Father was. Jesus's intention was to do the same acts as His Father, but not from the perspective of just trying to duplicate them. Rather, the motivation of His heart was the same as His Father's.

Someone who can change a lightbulb in their car isn't necessarily a mechanic. On the other hand, if I declare myself to be a mechanic yet am unable to change the lightbulb, you can doubt that I am who I say. My words alone prove nothing. It takes the consistent actions of the heart to truthfully declare who I really am.

Jesus always promoted His Father. He was so secure in that relationship that He could publicly tell people not to believe in Him if they didn't see Him doing the works of His Father.

That is a very bold statement for a man to make. Can you imagine a Christian leader today telling us not to believe a word they say unless they live in such a way as to prove their relationship with Father God?

Unfortunately, smooth talk gains followers. But it never sets a foundation for building anything eternal. A little wind working through the vocal cords produces speech, and speech is easily changeable, but godly character working through the heart produces actions that have an eternal message. The life of Jesus proved who He was. That life brings eternal expectation to us all. His life gave power to His words back then, and it still does today.

The apostle John wrote that Jesus perfectly did what His Father did:

> But Jesus said, "I tell you the truth, the Son can do nothing alone. The Son does only what he sees the Father doing, because the Son does whatever the Father does." (John 5:19, NCV)

What would it be like if we focused more on doing the deeds than talking the talk? Jesus's disciples were sent out and given more to do than they were given to say. It's true that both are equally important, but doing deeds requires a much greater connection to God than talking.

If God's Word is alive in me, it will be seen. If not, it's just dead letters.

Day Fifteen

WHAT'S WRONG WITH WONDERFUL WORKS?

Not every one that saith unto me, Lord, Lord, shall enter into the kingdom of heaven; but he that doeth the will of my Father which is in heaven. Many will say to me in that day, Lord, Lord, have we not prophesied in thy name? and in thy name have cast out devils? and in thy name done many wonderful works? (Matthew 7:21–22, KJV)

THERE ARE SO many wonderful things that we can do on our own, especially once we've received some training and learned a bit of self-discipline. Great things can be produced when we work with the knowledge we've acquired and it can give us a great sense of self-satisfaction. At times, it may be so wonderful that we're prompted to raise our hands and hopefully get some attention.

But if our motivation was to do the work all by ourselves, it has no eternal value. It was not motivated or directed by God. That doesn't make it bad; it just makes it temporary.

I have worked as a mechanic for most of my life and I derive great satisfaction from fixing things. I once met a man who needed help fixing his car that wouldn't start. He had tried many things and nothing got it started. I told him I would come over the next day to solve his problem. He looked at me questioningly and asked how I knew I could do it. I told him that I had often come up against trouble while working on unfamiliar equipment; when I couldn't figure out how to repair it, I prayed and asked God for help. Within a short time, the problem would be found and repaired.

The next morning, I came over and he opened the hood. Suddenly I felt prompted to do something I had never done before. I got a small jumper wire and connected the positive terminal on the coil to the positive post of the battery. He turned the key and started the car.

It ran perfectly. We were both shocked.

Something in me wanted to proudly pat myself on the back, but I could see something far greater than myself. I saw God working. He was using a temporary, dust-to-dust kind of vessel to show my new friend that not only was he seen and cared for, but God even cared about his car!

We are honoured when God chooses to work with us when He shows Himself to make a difference in someone's life. We are humbled and never promote the wonderful works we have done on our own.

Unfortunately, we easily say the words, "Lord, Lord," but we make life all about us and the wonderful things we do. The greatest satisfaction is in seeing Him do His work.

Day Sixteen

NEVER ABOVE HIM

The disciple is not above his master, nor the servant above his lord. It is enough for the disciple that he be as his master, and the servant as his lord. If they have called the master of the house Beelzebub, how much more shall they call them of his household? (Matthew 10:24–25, KJV)

SOCIAL STANDING BECOMES important when we compare ourselves with each other. If it's really possible to esteem others better than ourselves, as Jesus showed, then that's the way we must serve.

Let nothing be done through strife or vainglory; but in lowliness of mind let each esteem other better than themselves. Look not every man on his own things, but every man also on the things of others. Let this mind be in you, which was also in Christ Jesus... (Philippians 2:3–5, KJV)

My ability to esteem others above me is directly related to how I view myself. If I see myself as Jesus's disciple, or servant, I'll have no difficulty serving Him or anyone else. If I can't properly view and serve others, I don't have a view of Jesus that compels me to serve Him.

Jesus made it very clear that a disciple is not above his master. The disciple doesn't teach his master; he submits, always does what he is told, and learns. The disciple knows that he doesn't know and eagerly listens for instructions.

When I was learning to fly an airplane, my flight instructor always gave me clear instructions. When he had me doing stalls and spins, I never tried to tell him what to do. I listened and followed his instructions as perfectly as I could. I was always safe when I followed his instructions.

Eventually I was able to fly as well as my instructor, but I never saw myself as better than him. That attitude has stayed with me, even after many years of flying. I've kept the heart of a learner, especially when I was in the presence of my instructor.

Jesus calls us to relate to Him as our instructor. He will teach us all things and show us how to serve. Whether we're being honoured or dishonoured, we continue to serve even those considered to be the least important. That's how we honour our Master.

Day Seventeen

ABRAM'S CALL

Now the Lord said to Abram, "Go from your country, and from your relatives and from your father's house, to the land which I will show you; and I will make you into a great nation, and I will bless you, and make your name great; and you shall be a blessing; and I will bless those who bless you, and the one who curses you I will curse. And in you all the families of the earth will be blessed."

So Abram went away as the Lord had spoken to him; and Lot went with him. (Genesis 12:1–4, NASB)

SOME OF THE most difficult times in my life have been when God led us to leave what we were doing and move on to something new. The things we were doing had become familiar, rewarding, and successful; the new thing was never well-defined and the path to it was never very clear. That made it hard to leave and begin a new journey.

When God called Abram, it wasn't just a call to leave something behind. The call also included a description of what God intended to do with him.

God doesn't always do this. Sometimes it's just the simple call: "Follow Me."

But whether I know the purpose or not, I don't know the process to get there. Abram knew the purpose but didn't have a clue what the process would be except for taking the first step. He needed to leave his current place, and the people with him, to go someplace God would show him.

Abram did some pretty stupid stuff on that journey (see Genesis 12:11–41 for an example). God's grace worked to protect Abram and his family in that situation.

The greatest motivating factor in Abram's life was his faith in God, not the promise of blessings and having a great name. It's written in the book of Hebrews:

> By faith Abraham, when he was called to go out into a place which he should after receive for an inheritance, obeyed; and he went out, not knowing whither he went. By faith he sojourned in the land of promise, as in a strange country, dwelling in tabernacles with Isaac and Jacob, the heirs with him of the same promise: for he looked for a city which hath foundations, whose builder and maker is God. (Hebrews 11:8–10, KJV)

As Abram followed God, he didn't know where he was going, but he did know what he was looking for: a city encompassing all the reality of God.

When he began following at the age of seventy-five, he had no idea of the life experience ahead or what his character would be like by the time he died one hundred years later. We can only glimpse what he was like when God spoke to Isaac (Genesis 26:24) and used the words *"my servant Abraham."*

When God calls us to follow Him by faith, our character is changed.

Day Eighteen

A SERVANT TAKES ACTION

"Sir, if you think well of me, please stay awhile with me, your servant. I will bring some water so all of you can wash your feet. You may rest under the tree, and I will get some bread for you so you can regain your strength. Then you may continue your journey."
The three men said, "That is fine. Do as you said."
Abraham hurried to the tent where Sarah was and said to her, "Hurry, prepare twenty quarts of fine flour, and make it into loaves of bread." Then Abraham ran to his herd and took one of his best calves. He gave it to a servant, who hurried to kill it and to prepare it for food. Abraham gave the three men the calf that had been cooked and milk curds and milk. While they ate, he stood under the tree near them.
(Genesis 18:3–8, NCV)

ABRAHAM WAS A wealthy man with many servants. Earlier in life, he had encounters with God in which He clarified His promises. Abraham believed and followed in the journey that took him where God wanted him to be.

On any journey of faith, we will have encounters that encourage us and clarify the vision God has given us. As we follow along the path He has for us, our characters will change, motivating us to serve others as we serve God.

This is the condition Abraham was in when the Lord appeared to him. He saw three men and immediately invited them to stay for a while. He served them well, ensuring they were well-fed. Then he stood by, watching, to make sure everything was well. Abraham was actively engaged in working with others to make sure his guests were well-served. He proved that he served God by serving others.

Immediately after this happened, Abraham was told that he would have a son, even though he and his wife were past the age of having children.

The character of Abraham came into focus again a short time later when God was preparing to judge Sodom and Gomorrah. Because of Abraham's character, God informed him of His intentions.

> And the Lord said, Shall I hide from Abraham that thing which I do; seeing that Abraham shall surely become a great and mighty nation, and all the nations of the earth shall be blessed in him? For I know him, that he will command his children and his household after him, and they shall keep the way of the Lord, to do justice and judgment; that the Lord may bring upon Abraham that which he hath spoken of him. (Genesis 18:17–19, KJV)

It was a powerful thing for God to say that He knew Abraham. He knew the actions Abraham would take regarding his children and household. When God said that Abraham would command his children, He wasn't stating that Abraham would be so strong that he would force his children to obey. God knew that Abraham had a servant's heart and that his character would be strong enough to compel his children to follow. Abraham's character influenced his family long after he passed.

Strong, domineering people control others only when they are close. Humble servants like Abraham have a lasting influence even after they're gone.

Day Nineteen

BY FAITH, MOSES CHOSE

It was by faith that Moses, when he grew up, refused to be called the son of the king of Egypt's daughter. He chose to suffer with God's people instead of enjoying sin for a short time. He thought it was better to suffer for the Christ than to have all the treasures of Egypt, because he was looking for God's reward. It was by faith that Moses left Egypt and was not afraid of the king's anger. Moses continued strong as if he could see the God that no one can see. (Hebrews 11:24–27, NCV)

MOSES MADE SOME tough decisions. As a result, he went through very hard times. It would be interesting to know what went through his mind as he grew up in a very privileged class only to later discover his real family origin: slaves. As a child, he must have watched the interactions between the privileged and the slaves.

God must have put something in his heart to set him apart so he wouldn't fit in with the privileged family of the king. When he grew up, he made decisions that changed the course of his life. What compelled him to follow a path he knew would be filled with trouble? Why did he choose to suffer with the people of God rather than enjoy the riches of the king's family?

Whatever God put in his heart, Moses was greatly attracted to it. He willingly left everything else.

His choices were well-defined.

He could enjoy the pleasures of serving himself, gaining riches and social status and dominating others less fortunate. He would never have to be a servant to anyone.

Or he could join up with God's people, who suffered a lot. These people had been promised a future, but many died without ever receiving their promises. Their current condition was difficult. They suffered adversity and torment at the hands of those who ruled over them. They had no property and few human rights, but they were the ones God had chosen.

These were the ones Moses chose to identify with after considering both options. He became a servant of God and God stated the facts as He saw them.

> And he said, Hear now my words: If there be a prophet among you, I the Lord will make myself known unto him in a vision, and will speak unto him in a dream. My servant Moses is not so, who is faithful in all mine house. With him will I speak mouth to mouth... (Numbers 12:6–8, KJV)

We also have to make choices that will determine our lives and eternity. If we're wise, like Moses, we'll look at the options and choose the one with eternal value. It will lead us on a path of faithful service to God.

Day Twenty

HIS SERVANTS ARE NEVER ALONE

Verily, verily, I say unto you, Except a corn of wheat
fall into the ground and die, it abideth alone: but if it
die, it bringeth forth much fruit. He that loveth his life
shall lose it; and he that hateth his life in this world
shall keep it unto life eternal. If any man serve me,
let him follow me; and where I am, there shall also
my servant be: if any man serve me, him will my Father honour. (John 12:24–26, KJV)

WHEN GOD CREATED Adam in the Garden of Eden, He gave him
all the authority he needed to do his job. Adam enjoyed every godly provision. It was almost a perfect environment. In fact, he was
given only one little restriction: he couldn't eat of the tree of the
knowledge of good and evil. All the other trees were available if he
wanted them.

Then, as God looked over the situation, He knew something was
not good.

And the Lord God said, It is not good that the man
should be alone; I will make him an help meet for
him. (Genesis 2:18, KJV)

It's not good to be alone! God knows exactly how to fix it in every
situation.

Years ago, I was working for an outfitter in northern British Colombia. We guided hunters in very remote areas that could only be
accessed by airplane. One year, I got dropped off at a lake to prepare
a camp for some hunters. Tents had been dropped off but none had

been set up. This was a big job to do by myself! I would have to erect several tents, cut firewood, and prepare an outhouse.

Although more people would be coming the next day, for now I was alone.

It was midafternoon when I decided to sit under a tree and take a short break. The sun was shining, the lake was calm, and I was perfectly relaxed.

Suddenly I heard the most vicious scream I had ever heard, and it was coming from the branches of the tree I was sitting under. I jumped up and grabbed my rifle to protect myself. I felt extremely alone as I looked around, expecting to see a cougar or mountain lion. I had never felt so alone in all my life.

As I looked up into the tree, I encountered a beautiful mature bald eagle sitting beside a young one. I had never heard an eagle make such sounds before, so it was with quick relief that I realized it was only a bird.

It took a long time for me to get beyond my great sense of solitude.

God gave Adam a wife so he wouldn't be alone, and Jesus gave His followers a parable of what it takes for a kernel of wheat to get beyond the stage of being alone. When Jesus used the word alone, it meant more than just being on one's own; it also meant being stuck, unable to change. He explained that if anyone wanted to serve Him, they should follow Him. This means entering a place where one is never alone. A follower of Jesus is always with Him.

Our greatest connection comes as a result of following Jesus.

Day Twenty-One

CALEB HAD ANOTHER SPIRIT

Surely they shall not see the land which I sware unto their fathers, neither shall any of them that provoked me see it: but my servant Caleb, *because he had another spirit with him, and hath followed me fully,* him will I bring into the land whereinto he went; and his seed shall possess it. (Numbers 14:23–24, KJV, emphasis added)

OUR DIFFERENCES SET us apart. During the time my family and I lived in northern B.C., I walked almost everywhere. There were no cars, so there were no roads. But walking trails were everywhere. If we wanted to go somewhere that wasn't along the river, we had to walk.

I learned to more than walk. I learned to walk fast!

One winter, while walking with my friend Gary, who had come for a visit, we made our way along a trail with a bit of snow on it. He was taller than me and his legs were longer, but I could walk fast enough to keep up.

We were walking at a good speed when another friend of mine, Antoine, came up from behind and passed us. He had been born and raised in the area and could show us what fast walking was all about!

When we all got to the cabin we were heading for, Gary told Antoine, "I've never seen anybody walk so fast in my entire life!"

Antoine patted his legs. "You never met these kind of legs before."

We had to conclude that his legs were different.

The people Moses sent to spy out the Promised Land were different from each other. God had supernaturally brought them all out of Egypt, led them miraculously through the Red Sea, and given them everything they needed to get all the way to the land God had promised them. And now it was time to check out the land to see what it was like. What kind of people were there?

Moses gave them God's instructions: they were to check for some specific qualities of the land and the people. These twelve men were to bring back a report as well as some fruit of the land.

They all saw the same thing: a land flowing with milk and honey, and the people living there were very great—giants, in fact—and had fortified cities.

However, even though all twelve men were aware of the promises God had made them, they reached different conclusions. Ten of the men said it would be impossible to take the land because of how big the people were; they explained that the cities were well-built and fortified. On the other hand, Joshua and Caleb concluded that it would be no problem to take the land, since they were *"well able to overcome it"* (Numbers 13:30, KJV).

What made the difference? Why did Joshua and Caleb think differently? Why did some say it would be impossible while others felt they were well able to do it? Why did some see the people in the land as undefeatable giants while others saw them as easily defeatable?

It's important for us to know the answers to these questions because we will be like one of these groups. First of all, we must note that God identified Caleb as His servant. A servant has a different spirit, or expression of life, than others. This kind of servant follows the Master everywhere He goes.

God's promises had been made to all of Israel, but few received the benefit of those promises because they didn't follow as servants of God.

Day Twenty-Two

MY SERVANT JOB

And the Lord said unto Satan, Hast thou considered my servant Job, that there is none like him in the earth, a perfect and an upright man, one that feareth God, and escheweth evil? Then Satan answered the Lord, and said, Doth Job fear God for nought? Hast not thou made an hedge about him, and about his house, and about all that he hath on every side? thou hast blessed the work of his hands, and his substance is increased in the land. (Job 1:8–10, KJV)

JOB WASN'T SOME mythical person who someone decided to write a story about. He was a real person. He was introduced and identified as having excellent character.

There was a man in the land of Uz, whose name was Job; and that man was perfect and upright, and one that feared God, and eschewed evil. (Job 1:1, KJV)

Somehow he became aware of the one God. He had no part of the culture that worshipped the sun, moon, or stars. His focus and desire was on the one God who ruled supreme.

Whatever it was that awoke his awareness of God also drove him to serve Him with all his heart.

God noticed.

Satan also noticed.

Job wasn't aware that anyone had noticed. He just kept serving God and looking after his family's physical and spiritual needs. His character, as described by God, was gentle and reverent, turning away from evil.

Satan thought the only reason Job served God was for the personal benefit of himself and his family. Of course Satan would think that; that's the only way he can think. But it wasn't true of Job. Even after he lost everything and his wife told him to end it all, Job refused. While he may have been afraid of what life would be like without God, he hadn't ever served God for what he could get.

So why did Job serve God? He knew enough that he felt compelled to serve this One who was so great that nothing else compared.

Later, after all his trials were over, Job declared that before all these calamities he had only known God by what he heard. But afterward he declared that he could *see* Him. His servant's heart didn't change, but he benefited from a new perspective.

Could it be that the greatest, most perfect servants go through the greatest tests? While we don't serve God for our own personal benefit, we do get the greatest benefit. It's all because of Him!

Day Twenty-Three

JESUS THE PERFECT SERVANT

Here is my servant, the one I support. He is the one
I chose, and I am pleased with him. I have put my
Spirit upon him, and he will bring justice to all nations. He will not cry out or yell or speak loudly in the
streets. He will not break a crushed blade of grass or
put out even a weak flame. He will truly bring justice;
he will not lose hope or give up until he brings justice to the world. And people far away will trust his
teachings. (Isaiah 42:1–4, NCV)

WHILE JESUS WAS on the earth, He showed Himself to be a perfect
example of a servant of God. Isaiah had prophesied about what Jesus would be like as a servant on the earth, mentioning seven things
Jesus would not engage in on account of his servanthood. These
actions were connected to His voice, His actions, and His attitude.

Our voice is the tool we learn to use at first to bring attention to
ourselves. When babies need food, they cry until they get it. This a
natural, built-in tool that requires no training. The training we need is
how to avoid using it every time we want attention.

Many of our actions never need to be taught. Healthy infants
never need to be taught to grip a finger that's placed in their hand.
Has anyone ever taught a baby to put its hand in its mouth? There is
an urge in every child to reach out and touch everything it can reach,
often putting it in its mouth. The child has to be trained not to touch
certain things—for example, hot things cause pain.

Our attitudes spring from the condition of our hearts. When we
experience a lot of failure, we can lose hope and want to give up. We

no longer expect to succeed. Our high sense of entitlement can drive us to discouragement and depression when we encounter delays and difficulties.

Jesus came with no sense of entitlement. He knew that God had given Him everything He needed to live as a servant, and He perfectly followed His Father every day.

All the instincts we're born with naturally draw us to serve ourselves. We must be born again so the instincts that come from our heavenly Father are birthed within us. God will also put His Spirit on us, as He did for Jesus, allowing us to follow the example of Jesus.

I can live the life of a perfect servant, but I must choose God's way instead of my own.

Day Twenty-Four

JESUS EMPTIED HIMSELF

Let this mind be in you, which was also in Christ Jesus: who, being in the form of God, thought it not robbery to be equal with God: but made himself of no reputation, and took upon him the form of a servant, and was made in the likeness of men: and being found in fashion as a man, he humbled himself, and became obedient unto death, even the death of the cross. (Philippians 2:5–8, KJV)

PAUL HAD AN amazing ability to perfectly express the mindset of Jesus. The choices Jesus made while on the earth show that He knew perfectly why He had come. A few things were required of Him before He could do this. If He was going to be a perfect sacrifice and die on a cross, He would need to leave something behind... and pick up something else.

One thing was sure: God couldn't die, nor could He be killed. So Jesus would need to let go of His divinity and somehow be made in the same nature as a human being if He intended to be a sacrifice for sin.

Jesus clearly knew where He came from. He also understood His equality with God, who was His Father. But He didn't let these things get in His way of offering Himself as a perfect sacrifice and dying on the cross. It must have been great love for His Father, and us, that drove Him as He *"made himself of no reputation."*

He emptied Himself of who He was so He could pick up something else He desired. He couldn't be both at the same time. So He picked up the nature of a servant and became a human, like us.

However, that doesn't mean He did the things we do. Our human nature most often drives us to build upon those things that are highly valued while trying to let go of lesser qualities. Jesus did the opposite, letting go of the highest quality of life any being could have and picking up the characteristics of a servant. He never went back and never changed His mind. He stayed a servant until the end when He let Himself be nailed to a cross.

> Thinkest thou that I cannot now pray to my Father, and he shall presently give me more than twelve legions of angels? But how then shall the scriptures be fulfilled, that thus it must be? (Matthew 26:53–54, KJV)

Jesus could have changed His mind, but He knew what was required of Him. He had at His disposal more than seventy-two thousand angels if He wanted them. All He had to do was call.

But He didn't.

Our basic human nature strives to attain the highest possible status. This nature is our greatest obstacle, keeping us from taking the lower place that allows us to embrace our inner servant.

I want His mind, His way of thinking, so I can also experience the freedom of serving God perfectly.

Day Twenty-Five

INSTRUCTIONS FOR THE CALLED ONES

But when thou art bidden, go and sit down in the lowest room; that when he that bade thee cometh, he may say unto thee, Friend, go up higher: then shalt thou have worship in the presence of them that sit at meat with thee. For whosoever exalteth himself shall be abased; and he that humbleth himself shall be exalted. (Luke 14:10–11, KJV)

SOMETHING IN OUR human nature drives us to seek attention. This "Look at me!" attitude seems to motivate so many of our actions that we rarely notice other people, causing us to miss out on seeing the greatness in others. It also prevents us from seeing the broken and hurting ones who are close. Having an inflated view of myself causes me to minimize the greatness of others and criticize the broken and hurting when I see them.

At times, I've gone to Sunday morning breakfasts for homeless people. I'll never forget one Sunday morning when I did a short devotion just before breakfast. It all went well. Then we visited together as we ate.

Shortly after breakfast, I left to go to the church we normally attended. As I walked out the door, I encountered a man standing outside smoking a cigarette. He was one of the poor people who'd come for breakfast. I smelled the smoke and first thought, "Doesn't this man have any respect for others, or for this church as a gathering place?"

Then he noticed me.

"Hey buddy," he said. "What you said in there really got to me. I have to hurry up and finish this…" He held up his cigarette. "…so I can get back in there and hear what else they have to say."

Suddenly, I felt very ashamed of myself.

Later on, as I walked to the door of our usual church, I could almost imagine that same man smoking at our church door. This time my attitude was different. My heart had been corrected and humbled. I think I would have stood beside him as he finished his cigarette, then helped him find a seat beside me in church. Radical? Maybe. But it's only considered radical in light of what we would consider "normal" behaviour.

Jesus knew the importance of taking the lowest place. He did it perfectly.

> Wherefore God also hath highly exalted him, and given him a name which is above every name…
> (Philippians 2:9, KJV)

God knows how to perfectly exalt those who refuse to lift themselves up, and He does it publicly. In the same way, He can perfectly put down those who promote themselves rather than others.

If we will follow Him, we must do it perfectly, too. If we are to be exalted, let it be God who does it, not us.

HE CHOSE DAVID TO BE HIS SERVANT

He chose David to be his servant and took him from the sheep pens. He brought him from tending the sheep so he could lead the flock, the people of Jacob, his own people, the people of Israel. And David led them with an innocent heart and guided them with skillful hands. (Psalm 78:70–72, NCV)

GOD'S WAY OF doing things is often hard for us to understand, especially when He's just starting something. Years later, when we get the big picture, it usually makes sense. We don't have the same perspective as God.

When God caused Samuel to go out looking for the right person to anoint as king of Israel, Samuel was puzzled. God didn't seem to be looking for the tallest, best-looking, most impressive king. No, God's way is different.

But the Lord said to Samuel, "Don't look at how handsome Eliab is or how tall he is, because I have not chosen him. God does not see the same way people see. People look at the outside of a person, but the Lord looks at the heart." (1 Samuel 16:7, NCV)

Why would God choose a person who lived in the hills and watched sheep over someone from the big city who was highly educated, upper class, and popular?

Although God was looking for a king, He was really looking for a servant. He found in David a servant's heart. David had tenderheartedly served the lonely, often broken and dirty sheep when there was no one else around to help. That was the kind of servant God was looking for, someone to lead His people along His path.

David had an innocent heart, full of integrity, and skillful hands that worked with understanding and wisdom. People would know David because they could watch him. He lived his life in the open and was a safe man to follow.

But being safe doesn't mean he did everything perfectly. David probably made some mistakes as he took care of the sheep, leading them through the hills and valleys looking for water and green grass. We know he made some mistakes as king as well, but his heart always turned back to God.

There are times in our lives when it looks like we're doing nothing of significance. We're like David, just walking some lonely hills, trying to find enough water and grass to keep ourselves and maybe a few sheep alive.

Meanwhile, God is looking for a faithful, unknown, insignificant servant who has found great satisfaction while serving in an unseen place. This is the one God chooses. He knows this type of person can be trusted because he has developed an innocent heart and skillful hands.

Jesus said it perfectly. If we are wise, we will follow His example.

And whosoever shall exalt himself shall be abased;
and he that shall humble himself shall be exalted.
(Matthew 23:12, KJV)

Day Twenty-Seven

SAUL WAS NOT A SERVANT

He had a son named Saul, a handsome, young man. No man in Israel was more handsome than Saul. He stood a head taller than everyone else.

When some donkeys belonging to Saul's father Kish were lost, Kish told Saul, "Take one of the servants with you, and go look for the donkeys." (1 Samuel 9:2–3, GW)

WHEN ISRAEL FIRST became a nation in their own land, prophets judged the people and went to God for governmental instructions. Other nations had kings who ruled by decree. The people of Israel looked to these other nations and thought having a king would be a better way. It must have appeared to them that putting faith in a man they could see would be better than putting faith in a God they couldn't see.

The people also didn't like how the future looked. The prophet Samuel was getting old and his sons had some serious problems everyone knew about (1 Samuel 8:5–9). So they finally told Samuel that they wanted a king. They didn't have a clue what they were asking for, though, and Samuel was very unhappy about the request.

But since they wanted a king, God would give them exactly that.

Even though Samuel told them what this would be like, it didn't change their minds (1 Samuel 8:11–17). Samuel told them that this king would take their sons and appoint them to serve him. Over and over, Samuel said, "He will take… he will take… he will take." He concluded by telling the people that they would all be servants to the king.

Their hearts were set, so God gave them what they wanted. It wasn't God's choosing; it was the people who chose. They wouldn't get a king who served, but rather one they must serve.

Since God knows everything, He had just the kind of person for the job. His name was Saul. He was the tallest and best-looking man in the country. His family had enough wealth and status that when his father sent him out one day to look for their donkeys, he was told to bring a servant along with him.

Saul hadn't grown up as a servant. He grew up being served.

When the time came for Saul to be presented to the people as their king, he hid himself. But being shy is different from being humble. God did some great things for Saul, but he never had the heart of a servant. Rather, he needed to be served. He was so self-centred that he tried to destroy anyone who appeared to be better than him.

Finally, his self-centeredness led to him being rejected by God.

> And Samuel said unto Saul, I will not return with thee: for thou hast rejected the word of the Lord, and the Lord hath rejected thee from being king over Israel. (1 Samuel 15:26, KJV)

Any time God puts us in a place of prominence, our safest place will always be in the role of a servant.

Day Twenty-Eight

MY SERVANT JACOB

But thou, Israel, art my servant, Jacob whom I have chosen, the seed of Abraham my friend. Thou whom I have taken from the ends of the earth, and called thee from the chief men thereof, and said unto thee, Thou art my servant; I have chosen thee, and not cast thee away. Fear thou not; for I am with thee: be not dismayed; for I am thy God: I will strengthen thee; yea, I will help thee; yea, I will uphold thee with the right hand of my righteousness. (Isaiah 41:8–10, KJV)

IT'S AN HONOUR any time God puts His eye on a person and chooses them. It's always for a specific purpose at a specific time.

In grade school, we played games at recess. We would start with two captains choosing their teams. They took turns picking the people they wanted on their side. The people chosen first were either the captains' best friends or were very good at the game being played. It was always shameful to be the last one chosen, because it meant the captain didn't like you or you were a poor player.

God isn't like these grade school team captains. He reminded Israel, who He identified as His servant, that He had chosen him while he still had Jacob's nature. Jacob hadn't been trustworthy because life was all about him. But that changed after his encounter with God when they wrestled all night and he became crippled from the angel's touch (Genesis 32:27–28).

God told Israel twice in a very short time that he was His servant, and that he had been chosen. Then God assured him that he wouldn't be cast away.

Why did Israel need all this assurance from God? God had given Israel a great promise that he would lack for nothing. The promise was full and complete. Those words were powerfully reassuring.

A year after having a heart attack, while still having heart issues, I went to Belize to work as a program director for a six-week term. It was hot and we were very busy. After about two weeks, I was tired and weak. Since I didn't have the energy to keep going, I decided to return home.

The next morning, I started walking to the dining hall where we had staff meetings at six o'clock. I planned to let the staff know that due to my heart problems I would need to go home.

But just before I opened the door to go in, my cellphone dinged. I thought it was odd to get a message at that time of day, so I stopped to check it.

I was shocked. It was my verse of the day, from an app that didn't usually appear until much later in the day. I read these words:

Fear thou not; for I am with thee: be not dismayed; for I am thy God: I will strengthen thee; yea, I will help thee; yea, I will uphold thee with the right hand of my righteousness. (Isaiah 41:10, KJV)

It was God Himself talking to me. At that moment, I knew that I didn't need to go home. I could stay and finish the job God had sent me to do.

When God calls us to serve Him, the condition of our body doesn't determine whether we will succeed. Successful service is only possible when we embrace the promised provisions.

Day Twenty-Nine

THE SHEPHERD LEADS

Truly, truly I say to you, the one who does not enter by the door into the fold of the sheep, but climbs up some other way, he is a thief and a robber. But the one who enters by the door is a shepherd of the sheep. To him the doorkeeper opens, and the sheep listen to his voice, and he calls his own sheep by name and leads them out. (John 10:1–3, NASB)

WHEN THE SHEPHERD wants our attention, He calls us by name. This is a beautiful quality about Him. He never calls us by saying "Hey you!" His invitation to us is always personal. We're not called to follow Him as a group.

We all have a name and recognize when our name is spoken. Most babies recognize and respond to their names by the time they're eight months old, but some respond as early as four months. Somehow this is built in at birth and develops very quickly, especially when the name is spoken by a parent.

Our ability to respond when our name is called is an important part of building relationships with others. God made us that way, and it's also an important factor in our relationship with Him.

The apostle John finished his writing to the church by giving them some interesting instructions:

But I trust I shall shortly see thee, and we shall speak face to face. Peace be to thee. Our friends salute thee. *Greet the friends by name.* (3 John 14, KJV, emphasis added)

God knows all of His servants by name.

> So the Lord said to Moses, "I will also do this thing that you have spoken; for you have found grace in My sight, and I know you by name." (Exodus 33:17, NKJV)

It's no small thing when God tells a man that He knows him by name. God had this connection with us before we were born. He knows what name to use when He calls us to follow Him, to leave behind the safe and secure structure of the proverbial sheepfold. While in the fold, the sheep are safe. They can lie down or walk around without danger.

There is a time and purpose for being in the fold, but it's only a short time. The Shepherd calls us by name to come out of this safe resting place. As one of His sheep, we recognize His voice and follow Him wherever He goes. There will be times of great danger, when it's dark and the path is steep. Other voices will also call us, but our only safety is in perfectly following the voice of the Shephard.

We never have to worry about the Shepherd silently abandoning us, leaving us to perish. He will never forsake us. Our jeopardy is that we sometimes choose not to follow where He leads. We grow fearful of the journey. Sometimes we look around and see more pleasant paths.

Learning to know and follow His voice will always bring us to the safest and most rewarding life anyone could have. When He calls your name, follow Him!

Day Thirty

THE SHEPHERD EJECTS

And when he putteth forth his own sheep, he goeth before them, and the sheep follow him: for they know his voice. And a stranger will they not follow, but will flee from him: for they know not the voice of strangers. (John 10:4–5, KJV)

WE CREATE DIFFICULTIES when we compare ourselves to each other in terms of the way God deals with us. Often our narrowmindedness excludes us from being able to see God working in our lives, as well as the lives of others.

First Jesus told the parable of the good shepherd bringing his sheep out of the fold to take them on a journey someplace where they'd be fed, watered, and able to grow. He starts by calling out the names of sheep. As they respond, he gently leads them out of the fold.

Then He painted a totally different picture.

The second picture is totally different. He speaks of sheep being ejected from the fold. The original Hebrew word translated as *"putteth forth"* refers to being cast out. There is nothing gentle or soft about this. It's hard, dramatic, and radical. This can take the form of afflictions that force us to change.

Much of modern Christianity focuses on the external blessings of prosperity and personal promotion. From this perspective, our lives revolve around ourselves and the pleasures we can enjoy. But none of this helps us stay on the path God has for us. In fact, these things actually distract us from serving God. Instead we can follow the desires of our own hearts.

It can be harder and harder to hear the good shepherd calling to us as our own voices drown him out. We can end up choosing our own paths, ones that may appear right in our own eyes.

God has an answer for our dilemma. David wrote about it in the book of Psalms after he went through some very difficult times.

> Before I was afflicted I went astray: but now have I kept thy word. Thou art good, and doest good; teach me thy statutes. (Psalm 119:67–68, KJV)

The whole purpose of being given an affliction, of being taken out of our comfort zones, is to make us focus on no voice other than the shepherd's.

David concluded that God is good and does good things. He never makes a mistake.

Whether I'm following Him because I've heard Him call my name, or I'm following Him after having been ejected from my secure place, the sound of His voice will lead me. As I follow that path, all the plans He has for my life will be fulfilled. Finally, at the end of that path, I will hear Him say, "Well done!"

Day Thirty-One

FOLLOW HIS EXAMPLE

For what glory is it, if, when ye be buffeted for your faults, ye shall take it patiently? but if, when ye do well, and suffer for it, ye take it patiently, this is acceptable with God. For even hereunto were ye called: because Christ also suffered for us, leaving us an example, that ye should follow his steps... (1 Peter 2:20–21, KJV)

ONE OF THE best ways to learn how to do something is to watch someone else do it. For several years, I worked as shop foreman in an RV shop. I worked with apprentices for whose training I was responsible. The most enjoyable and effective way to train them was to get my hands dirty as I showed them how to troubleshoot and fix difficult mechanical problems. Later, when these same problems showed up in other units, the young mechanics could find and resolve the problem by themselves.

This wouldn't have worked as well if I had just sat in my office and explained to them what to do. I would have stayed clean in my nice office chair, but there would have been no example for them to follow.

Jesus had no desire to stay clean in His office chair. He had much higher goals that required Him to experience the dirt and pain of life. We needed to see Him successfully navigate the difficulties of life while pleasing God in the process.

Peter tells us to take our difficulties patiently. This isn't about suffering the consequences of our mistakes, but rather going through suffering without having made a mistake. Totally unfair!

God knew we would need an example of how to remain firm under the pain of accusations while having done no wrong. Jesus showed us how to do this in a way that is acceptable to God. Even the best apprentice wouldn't have figured this out by himself.

This wasn't written so we would know how to respond *if* this happens. We are told that this is what He has called us to do. This isn't a general call. The original language strongly implies that this is why He called us by name.

If you have answered the call to follow Jesus, you will accompany Him as you take these steps that are so pleasing to God.

Day Thirty-Two

GOD'S PURPOSE

Yet it was our weaknesses he carried; it was our sorrows that weighed him down. And we thought his troubles were a punishment from God, a punishment for his own sins! But he was pierced for our rebellion, crushed for our sins. He was beaten so we could be whole. He was whipped so we could be healed. All of us, like sheep, have strayed away. We have left God's paths to follow our own. Yet the Lord laid on him the sins of us all. (Isaiah 53:4–6, NLT)

WHENEVER GOD DOES something, there is more than a reason for it. It has a purpose. There is an action for it to accomplish, not just an explanation. Actions are much easier to see and understand than explanations.

Years ago, my wife and I visited a place where pottery is made. We were standing on a balcony to see out over the room where several people were working with clay while it spun on a flat wheel.

A man had just cleaned off his wheel and was getting ready to start with a new lump of clay. He reached into a bucket beside him and with both hands took out a fairly large piece of wet clay. I watched him work the clay with his hands.

Then, with full force, using both hands, he slammed the clay onto the spinning table in front of him. That action was totally unexpected and I was shocked.

"Why did you hit it so hard?" I shouted out to him.

With both hands on the clay that was spinning in front of him, and without even looking up, he answered: "So it stays on the wheel."

At that moment, I understood the purpose of his action.

This brought back a painful situation in my life I had gone through and always wondered about. Why had it happened? Now I understood the purpose: it had happened so I would stay on the proverbial wheel while God formed me.

Jesus also stayed on the wheel as He went through many painful experiences on the earth. He remained faithful in every difficulty, knowing that it would accomplish the purpose of His Father: to make a way for each of us to be cleanly reconciled to God. Jesus served His Father perfectly and made a way so we could get back to the Father.

Now the question I must answer is simple: will I stay on the wheel and serve Him perfectly so others can benefit?

Day Thirty-Three

MY BELOVED'S VOICE

> The voice of my beloved! behold, he cometh leaping upon the mountains, skipping upon the hills. My beloved is like a roe or a young hart: behold, he standeth behind our wall, he looketh forth at the windows, shewing himself through the lattice. My beloved spake, and said unto me, Rise up, my love, my fair one, and come away. (Song of Soloman 2:8–10, KJV)

THE SHULAMITE WOMAN in this passage was enthralled with the one she loved. Soloman wrote a lot about the relationship she had with her lover. When she talked about her lover's captivating voice, she described it as far more than the sound she heard when he spoke. It was the fullness of the sound he made as he moved. She could hear him as he leapt on the distant mountains and skipped on the surrounding hills. She had been close enough to see and hear him as he went about doing all these things and recognized the familiar sounds. She knew where he was because she could hear him even when she couldn't see him.

This is important for us, too. When we become familiar with our close friends, or our spouse, we recognize the sound of their footsteps. Without question, we know when they're close and walking around.

While I lay in a hospital bed after suffering a heart attack, I recognized when my wife walked into the room even when the curtain was pulled around my bed. Other times I recognized her voice as she talked to someone in the hall. I couldn't understand every word she spoke, but I knew she was close.

To clearly hear and understand her words, though, something needed to happen. The distance between us needed to change.

The same principle applies to our relationship with our Beloved, the Shepherd. I must get closer to understand His words. The call of the Beloved is for us to rise up from everything that holds us down and come closer. As we move close, the distance grows between us and our former way of living. The power of His invitation captivates us, just like it did the Shulamite woman.

As I follow the voice of the one who called me by His grace, my intense love for Him will motivate me to leave everything behind and never look back. There is so much beauty in His invitation: *"Rise up, my love, my fair one, and come away."*

Day Thirty-Four

THE STRANGERS

Son of man, prophesy against the shepherds, the leaders of Israel. Give them this message from the Sovereign Lord: what sorrow awaits you shepherds who feed yourselves instead of your flocks. Shouldn't shepherds feed their sheep? You drink the milk, wear the wool, and butcher the best animals, but you let your flocks starve. You have not taken care of the weak. You have not tended the sick or bound up the injured. You have not gone looking for those who have wandered away and are lost. Instead, you have ruled them with harshness and cruelty. So my sheep have been scattered without a shepherd, and they are easy prey for any wild animal. They have wandered through all the mountains and all the hills, across the face of the earth, yet no one has gone to search for them. (Ezekial 34:2–6, NLT)

HOW CAN I know the difference between the good Shepherd and the stranger who claims to be a shepherd, but isn't? Jesus said,

And a stranger will they not follow, but will flee from him: for they know not the voice of strangers. (John 10:5, KJV)

Obviously, those who follow the good Shepherd know when it's the voice of a stranger. They react accordingly. It's not about trying to ignore him; they run away from and shun him.

A stranger is more than just someone I don't know. It could be someone from a different country and totally different culture. They could have nothing in common with my good Shepherd.

God made it clear to Ezekial that there was a difference between those who called themselves shepherds and those who actually were shepherds. They had different cultures. One culture consumed everything for themselves and gave nothing, while the other gave everything and consumed nothing for themselves.

As we live our lives doing what God put us here to do, we must maintain an awareness of the good Shepherd by consciously choosing to stay close, watch, and listen for Him.

There is no better way to become acquainted with someone than to be in their presence. I need to avoid being in the company of those who only feed themselves, lest I find rest in their culture.

I never want my lifestyle to cause me to stop seeing and touching the weak, sick, and injured, or stop rescuing those who are lost. This is where the good Shepherd will be.

Day Thirty-Five

THE SERVANT'S MOTIVATION

Jesus knowing that the Father had given all things into his hands, and that he was come from God, and went to God; he riseth from supper, and laid aside his garments; and took a towel, and girded himself. After that he poureth water into a bason, and began to wash the disciples' feet, and to wipe them with the towel wherewith he was girded. (John 13:3–5, KJV)

JESUS'S ACTIONS SET Him apart from everyone around Him. His life was so different that people noticed Him everywhere He went. He didn't try to make Himself shine to get attention. He was noticeable partly because of who He was and what He knew He had. God had given all things into His hands.

But that didn't produce any arrogance or expectations of special treatment in Him. He also knew where He came from and where He was going. People are attracted to people who have that kind of security because it usually guarantees success in the journey of life.

To successfully get where I'm traveling to, I must be aware of these things. I must have everything I need to get there. I must know where I'm going and where I came from. I'll never get my GPS to show me how to get somewhere without also entering a starting point. It doesn't matter if I'm walking, running, driving, flying, or travelling by any other means.

These things are very important because they drive my actions just like they drove Jesus.

Jesus's actions demonstrate a perfect example of someone who's totally secure in what He has, where He's going, and where He came from.

John described it well. Jesus finished His actions by washing and wiping the disciples' feet. This was the job of the lowest servant. The master of the house would have had someone other than himself do it.

How different would our world be today if everyone were secure enough to take the place of a servant? How different would our churches be if everyone involved were to live as a servant? This has to start somewhere, so I must ask myself this question: how different will my world be when I become secure enough to be a servant, willing to wash and wipe feet?

SERVE WITH GLADNESS

> Serve the Lord cheerfully. Come into his presence with a joyful song. Realize that the Lord alone is God. He made us, and we are his. We are his people and the sheep in his care. Enter his gates with a song of thanksgiving. Come into his courtyards with a song of praise. Give thanks to him; praise his name. (Psalm 100:2–4, GW)

THE FIRST STATEMENT David makes here is to serve the Lord cheerfully. As I give my life in service to God, the only way to find fulfilment is to do it cheerfully. God has no desire for me to serve Him if I'm motivated by some legal obligation, experiencing emptiness and guilt when things don't go as expected.

This is how many religious leaders lived in biblical times. Their emptiness drove them to legislate strict rules of behaviour. They thought their obedience to the fine details would prove their service and devotion to God, but that's not how we are to serve God. They saw a dead law, not a living God.

David explained how to do it perfectly in the Psalms.

I've had jobs I didn't enjoy. Every day was the same. I went to work because I had made a commitment to the boss and I needed the paycheck.

I've also had jobs that were very enjoyable. These were satisfying. I could go to work cheerfully every day and do my work well because my heart was connected to it and the people I worked with. It was very rewarding.

When we answer the call to serve the Lord, it will primarily be for one of two reasons.

The first is that our brain and intellect direct us. We read the Bible to learn how God wants us to serve Him. Then we obey out of obligation, hoping to avoid any condemnation or guilt. Drudgery and unfulfillment soon follow and God seems a long way off.

The second is much more exciting. We answer the call to serve as a result of knowing intimacy with the one we serve. As a result, our hearts are connected to the work because we're connected to the one we're working for.

I will serve cheerfully when I know how perfectly He cares for me, and that I belong to Him. His care for me is perfect, so I cheerfully serve Him with a perfect heart.

GIVE FROM YOUR HEART

Each of you should give as you have decided in your heart to give. You should not be sad when you give, and you should not give because you feel forced to give. God loves the person who gives happily. (2 Corinthians 9:7, NCV)

THERE ARE THREE kinds of things I can give away: my stuff, my time, and my life. The things I clutch tightly to myself will be the hardest to give up.

I have easily given away some of my stuff when I knew I could easily replace it, or when I didn't need it anymore. But I would lend out the things that were important to me, expecting them to be returned. I keep the most valuable things to myself because it's too hard to let them go.

Giving away my time is different since I only have so much of it, and the demands of my day can often use it up. I have no time to give because there's none left. The only way I could give away time would be to eliminate some scheduled activity, which is difficult because it's hard to let go of what I do.

My life is the most difficult of all to give away because it's more than what I have and what I do; it's who I am. It's my name, my identity, the sum total of all I have and all I do. It would take great love to give my life.

One of the most impactful verses in the Bible is John 3:16:

> For God so loved the world, that he gave his only begotten Son, that whosoever believeth in him should

not perish, but have everlasting life. For God sent not his Son into the world to condemn the world; but that the world through him might be saved. (John 3:16–17, KJV)

His love, which was perfect, stimulated Him to the action of giving. He didn't just give something out of His perfect garden; He gave something of Himself—His only Son.

Our eternity is changed when we believe in Jesus, the one God gave us, because of the love that motivated Him to give. My relationship with Jesus will give me the greatest ability to give my life, all because I love.

My future is beautifully secured when love motivates me to give up my temporary life to serve the eternal Shepherd.

Day Thirty-Eight

YOU CAN ONLY SERVE ONE

No servant can serve two masters: for either he
will hate the one, and love the other; or else he will
hold to the one, and despise the other. Ye cannot
serve God and mammon. And the Pharisees also,
who were covetous, heard all these things: and
they derided him. And he said unto them, Ye are
they which justify yourselves before men; but God
knoweth your hearts: for that which is highly esteemed among men is abomination in the sight of
God. (Luke 16:13–15, KJV)

IT'S RECORDED MANY times in the Bible that Jesus used the
words "You cannot..." When He used these words, He was factu-
ally stating that something was impossible. It could not be done by
anyone.

When He said, *"No man can serve two masters,"* He was saying that it's impossible. He wasn't declaring a commandment. The
intensity and loyalty of true service make it impossible to serve two
masters. It would be like trying to go up and down at the same time,
or forward and backward. Jesus wasn't trying to be radical; He was
being real.

Unfortunately, we easily become like the Pharisees, whose focus
was always on themselves. They complicated truth by twisting it in
so many ways that it became impossible to follow. Basically, their
only god was themselves, and they took great care to serve that god.
Luke wrote that they were covetous—greedy, grabbing for anything
that would add to their wealth and religious status.

It's no wonder they had a terrible response to the truth Jesus declared. Luke said that they derided Him, which means they minimized Him and tried to convince others that Jesus was totally out of touch with truth.

How could they have been so stupid? Maybe they were so self-centred that they really believed they could serve God by serving themselves. But Jesus was right and they were wrong.

Great freedom and joy are found when I believe that what Jesus said is true. I stop trying to live the life that Jesus said was impossible. I'm no longer motivated, like the Pharisees, to seek material wealth or religious approval.

Freedom from myself sets me in a place where I can gleefully serve the Lord. This is the life that is possible.

Day Thirty-Nine

NOT BY OURSELVES

We are not saying that we can do this work our-selves. It is God who makes us able to do all that we do. He made us able to be servants of a new agreement from himself to his people. This new agreement is not a written law, but it is of the Spirit. The written law brings death, but the Spirit gives life. (2 Corinthians 3:5–6, NCV)

PAUL LIVED MANY years as a Pharisee, priding himself in who he was and what he could do. However, that all changed during an encounter with Jesus (Acts 26:13–18) when he saw a light and heard a voice. That's why he could write, and honestly believe, the above verses.

During this encounter, he lost his ability to go anywhere or do anything. He couldn't even stand on his own two feet. He could only lie on the ground and listen as Jesus gave him instructions. He couldn't get up until Jesus told him to.

This must have been very humbling for Paul, who at that time was called Saul. He lost all control over himself and the men around him. His response was very simple.

And I said, Who art thou, Lord? And he said, I am Jesus whom thou persecutest. But rise, and stand upon thy feet: for I have appeared unto thee for this purpose, to make thee a minister and a witness both of these things which thou hast seen, and of those things in the which I will appear unto thee... (Acts 26:15–16, KJV)

Paul's first encounter with Jesus set the stage for him to get acquainted with Him. Jesus didn't just introduce Himself by name and stop with that. He added the detail that Paul had been persecuting him. Those words must have torn into Paul's heart.

As Jesus continued to speak, Jesus told Paul to rise. He made it clear to Paul that the important thing to do now was to get up. There was no condemnation or shame for what had been done. It was about changing to become a new person with a new job despite the past.

The call to serve is always clear. When Jesus told Paul that His reason for appearing was to make him a minister, Paul would have had no feeling of great importance or anticipation of being in a special class. He knew the meaning of the word Jesus used. It meant that the whole intention of this encounter was to make him a subordinate, like slaves rowing a boat for a master while their feet were shackled to the floor. If the boat sank, they went with it, for they could be easily replaced.

Paul said yes and became a whole new man! He discovered that God was able to change him and give him the ability to do things that would have otherwise been impossible. He humbly stated, *"He made us able to be servants..."*

Lord, help us to become able servants.

Day Forty

ONLY WITH HIM

Abide in me, and I in you. As the branch cannot bear fruit of itself, except it abide in the vine; no more can ye, except ye abide in me. I am the vine, ye are the branches: He that abideth in me, and I in him, the same bringeth forth much fruit: for without me ye can do nothing. (John 15:4–5, KJV)

WE CAN DO so many things on our own that it becomes easy to think too highly of ourselves. I often don't want others helping me as I work because their presence can complicate the job. Sometimes it's true that others do complicate our jobs, but this definitely isn't true in our work as servants of God.

When I complete a job by myself, I get all the credit for it. If I work alongside others, I have to share the reward. And there are times when I work with someone else on a job and realize I could have never done it alone. The other person had information and skills I didn't have; I got the benefit of those skills and gained knowledge as we worked together.

While it's true that we can know what we know and become successful, it's also true that we don't know what we don't know. That can be deadly.

But if we can at least admit that there are things we can't do, things we don't know, we open the door to receive help from the One who knows all and can do all. The sooner we learn that without Him we can do nothing, the sooner we will be motivated to find an abiding place in Him.

Jesus calls us to abide in Him. This is different than the call to come to Him. Many people came to Jesus to get something they needed, including important things like healing and deliverance. They got what they needed and left.

The call for us to abide in Him is a call to come and stay. It's not about getting something for ourselves and leaving; it's about being changed and staying so our lives produce something others can benefit from. The only way I can serve the Lord for the benefit of others is by abiding in Him. Then He abides in me and much fruit gets picked and enjoyed by others. That fruit can never spoil because it's eternal.

> So then neither is he that planteth any thing, neither
> he that watereth; but God that giveth the increase.
> (1 Corinthians 3:7, KJV)

When much fruit is produced in my life, it's because God Himself has increased in my life. The greatest freedom in life is realized when I become nothing and God becomes everything. Then my service to Him will be perfect.

Day Forty-One

WALK IN LOVE

Be ye therefore followers of God, as dear children; and walk in love, as Christ also hath loved us, and hath given himself for us an offering and a sacrifice to God for a sweetsmelling savour. (Ephesians 5:1–2, KJV)

YEARS AGO, A friend told me that any time you read the word "therefore" in the Bible, you need to find out what it's "there for," because there is a reason. So when I read, *"Be ye therefore followers of God, as dear children; and walk in love,"* I needed to look back at what was written previously to understand the reason for calling followers of God to walk in love.

This is what he had just written, and it shows us the reason:

And be ye kind one to another, tenderhearted, forgiving one another, even as God for Christ's sake hath forgiven you. (Ephesians 4:32, KJV)

Our predominate actions and reactions unfortunately prove that we need to be told to be kind, tenderhearted, and forgiving. At times in my life, I've gotten irritated when a traffic light changed to red just before I got through the intersection—or worse yet, when someone ahead of me at a traffic light didn't go immediately when the light changed to green. It might only be a delay of a few seconds, but I would react with anything but kindness, tender-heartedness, or forgiveness. If this attitude goes unchecked, it eventually develops into violence.

This call to be a follower of God and walk in love is anchored in the fact that God has forgiven us in response to what Jesus did. Jesus not only forgave me; He showed me what it takes to be forgiving. Forgiving is more than an action. It's also the attitude that motivates the action. If I have a kind and tender heart, I'll never have difficulty forgiving anyone. I'll quickly and easily forgive the big offenders, as well as slow drivers ahead of me.

Jesus gave Himself, all of Himself, to His Father. His actions produced an attractive aroma that draws us to Him. As I follow the footsteps of Jesus, that same aroma is still being produced, attracting attention to the One who did it first.

Day Forty-Two

NOT MY WILL

There he told them, "Pray that you will not give in to temptation."

He walked away, about a stone's throw, and knelt down and prayed, "Father, if you are willing, please take this cup of suffering away from me. Yet I want your will to be done, not mine." Then an angel from heaven appeared and strengthened him. He prayed more fervently, and he was in such agony of spirit that his sweat fell to the ground like great drops of blood.

At last he stood up again and returned to the disciples, only to find them asleep, exhausted from grief. "Why are you sleeping?" he asked them. "Get up and pray, so that you will not give in to temptation." (Luke 22:40–46, NLT)

LIFE'S LESSONS ARE best learned from those who have successfully navigated the issues that distract us and cause us to fail. Jesus knew why He was here and had learned how to be successful in that mission.

As He faced the reality of going to the cross, the greatest test anyone could face, He took His disciples to a familiar place. Here He told them what to do and showed them how to do it. He told them to do exactly what He was doing. The instructions sounded fairly simple: *"Pray that you will not give in to temptation."* This was about more than just repeating some nice-sounding, familiar phrases. It was the cry of a committed heart, determined to do what was right while knowing the pain that would come as a result.

The driving force for Jesus didn't come from a commandment or expectation from God. These are strong motivators, but they're not what motivated Jesus to pray.

David wrote about it in the Psalms. Jesus had delight in doing the things that delighted His Father, God. Jesus's greatest pleasure was in doing the things that brought pleasure to His Father.

> Then said I, Lo, I come: in the volume of the book it
> is written of me, I delight to do thy will, O my God:
> yea, thy law is within my heart. (Psalm 40:7–8, KJV)

Jesus was conscious of His desire to do the things that pleased His Father. He was also aware of another desire pulling Him in the opposite direction. He had to choose which way He would go. Sleeping wouldn't resolve this issue. He would have to get up and pray if He was going to get what He needed to avoid giving in to the temptation.

Jesus was successful in every temptation.

I must learn to get up and pray if I intend not to give in to the temptations that come to me.

Day Forty-Three

KNOW WHO YOU FOLLOW

He showed you things so you would know that the Lord is God, and there is no other God besides him. He spoke to you from heaven to teach you. He showed you his great fire on earth, and you heard him speak from the fire. Because the Lord loved your ancestors, he chose you, their descendants, and he brought you out of Egypt himself by his great strength. He forced nations out of their land ahead of you, nations that were bigger and stronger than you were. The Lord did this so he could bring you into their land and give it to you as your own, and this land is yours today. (Deuteronomy 4:35–38, NCV)

TRAVELING IN OUR world today is easy. With all the electronic devices and apps at our disposal, it only takes seconds for us to get detailed instructions for how to get around every curve and corner along our journey. We also can determine the total distance and final arrival time.

Unfortunately, while our apps can quickly tell us how to get to the places we want to go, they have never been there themselves. They only pass on preprogrammed data that may or may not be correct. I know because I've gotten lost following the instructions. I must know the way and have the power to get there.

While flying in northern Yukon and Alaska, I used a LORAN (LOng RAnge Navigation) receiver to navigate. It was developed in the U.S. during World War Two and worked by receiving signals from different radio stations, hundreds of miles apart, and computing time delays between signals as I travelled. It worked quite well, so I trusted it.

However, while flying over some mountains one day it started giving random indications before the screen went blank. Later I found out that these mountains were known to have uranium. Somehow this messed up the radio signals. The LORAN lost my trust and I was very careful about following its indications after that.

Following God's instructions is totally different. He showed Israel evidence so they could know He was God and there was no other God besides Him. He actually spoke from heaven, through the fire, to teach them. He successfully led them out of very strong nations that had held them captive as slaves. They would never have known the way, or had the power to get out of those situations.

Once God had brought them out of captivity, He also proved that He could bring them in to the Promised Land, because one is not harder than the other. If I fail to get to where God wants me to be, it won't be the fault of the One giving directions and leading me; it will be that I failed to follow Him and His directions.

Our challenge is to know His voice and follow Him. He will always bring us home where we belong.

Day Forty-Four
OPTIONS

Now therefore fear the Lord, and serve him in sincerity and in truth: and put away the gods which your fathers served on the other side of the flood, and in Egypt; and serve ye the Lord. And if it seem evil unto you to serve the Lord, choose you this day whom ye will serve; whether the gods which your fathers served that were on the other side of the flood, or the gods of the Amorites, in whose land ye dwell: but as for me and my house, we will serve the Lord. And the people answered and said, God forbid that we should forsake the Lord, to serve other gods...
(Joshua 24:14–16, KJV)

OUR RELATIONSHIPS GROW successfully when we relate with integrity, with our hearts motivating us to be truthful in every interaction. On the other hand, if a relationship is driven by obedience to a commandment, all it takes is a directive for obedience to produce an action. No integrity or heart involvement is needed. On the outside, both relationships look alike, but inside they are opposite. One is dead and one is alive.

God's desire for relationship with us is the same as His desire for relationship with Israel. Joshua expressed it perfectly in his call for the people to fear the Lord and serve Him. This wasn't a call to serve Him because of fear of what would happen if they didn't.

However, this fear is real and valuable when it motivates us in the right direction. Without it, we can easily go the wrong direction. We could define this valuable fear as extreme reverence that comes from knowing God is always perfectly and completely in control of everything that was, and is, and is to come—and we are not.

David said it perfectly:

> Sin speaks to the wicked in their hearts. They have no fear of God. They think too much of themselves so they don't see their sin and hate it. (Psalm 36:1–2, NCV)

This valuable fear not only motivates me to serve the Lord but also stops me from thinking too much of myself, keeping me from elevating my ways and minimizing God's ways. We cannot serve the Lord and some other god at the same time. The one I choose to serve will be the one I have extreme reverence for.

God forbid that we should forsake the Lord to serve ourselves.

Day Forty-Five

TO LIVE WELL

Ye shall observe to do therefore as the Lord your God
hath commanded you: ye shall not turn aside to the
right hand or to the left. Ye shall walk in all the ways
which the Lord your God hath commanded you, that
ye may live, and that it may be well with you, and
that ye may prolong your days in the land which ye
shall possess. (Deuteronomy 5:32–33, KJV)

WHEN I CONSIDER some of the current definitions of success, most
of them aren't as complete as the one God gave Israel. Our modern
instructions are also different than God's instructions. God gave His
instructions so *"that ye may live."* This is about more than just having
a heartbeat; it's about being constantly revived for a purpose. The
purpose is *"that it may be well with you, and that ye may prolong
your days in the land which ye shall possess."*

Not everything that happens to us in life is pleasant, but there is
a way it can all be well with us. Paul said it this way:

Not that I speak in respect of want: for I have learned,
in whatsoever state I am, therewith to be content.
(Philippians 4:11, KJV)

This doesn't mean his experiences were peaceful. Many of them
were violent and painful. But Paul remained in a place of contentment. All was well with him. Through it all, he never stopped abiding
in the peace he possessed.

In this world, we will have difficulties that require changes and
movement in our lives. In the mid-nineties, I leased a gas station in

central Yukon. It was a good lease with the potential for purchase, so we set up a mobile home on the property and prepared for a long stay. Sometimes the days were long and finances were tight, but we always regained our strength and financial success. Things went well for us!

That is, until one day when we were informed that another company had bought the property and would take over at the end of our lease, which was only about a month away. We were surprised, since we had been assured of an extension of the lease agreement.

Shortly afterward, the new company offered to have us continue to run the business and live in our house on the property.

That, too, changed just seven days before the new company took over. They notified me that I needed to have all my belongings off the property before the ownership changed hands. That meant getting all my tools and equipment out of the shop. More than that, it meant I had to move a house, greenhouse, and chicken house all in seven days. We worked almost day and night to complete the work, but we got it done.

It was hard, but I learned some lessons.

Obeying God and not turning aside doesn't ensure that all our experiences will go smoothly and we'll never get booted from our physical residence. These promises all relate to things eternal, yet they bring contentment in the temporary, physical, and sometimes chaotic dealings of our daily lives.

There are eternal benefits for me if I stay in agreement with God's plan for me, never turning to go my own way.

LOVE DIRECTS ME

Thou shalt not hearken unto the words of that prophet, or that dreamer of dreams: for the Lord your God
proveth you, to know whether ye love the Lord your
God with all your heart and with all your soul. Ye
shall walk after the Lord your God, and fear him, and
keep his commandments, and obey his voice, and
ye shall serve him, and cleave unto him. (Deuteronomy 13:3–4, KJV)

LOVE IS A very strong motivator. It's like a magnet that draws me to
something I like while pushing me away from things I don't like. It's
the same with food. I fill my plate with the food I like best but take
very little of things I don't like. My reasons don't matter. I might like
a food because of the taste or because I know it's healthy. But one
thing remains consistent: me.

This is why we must be proven. It could also be said this way:
our lives must be carefully tested so we know the direction of our
love. These can be long and difficult times or short events that open
our eyes to who we really are. The result of being proven is that we
learn something about ourselves we didn't know before.

That's why David prayed this prayer:

Judge me, O Lord; for I have walked in mine integrity: I have trusted also in the Lord; therefore I shall
not slide. Examine me, O Lord, and prove me; try my
reins and my heart. (Psalm 26:1–2, KJV)

David wanted to know for sure that his relationship with the Lord wasn't all about himself, but that the motivation of his heart was all for God. He wanted to know that his love for God was more about giving to God than getting from Him.

This is what God wanted for Israel and what He wants for us today. Paul described love in great detail to the Corinthian church, but one small part stands out:

> Doth not behave itself unseemly, seeketh not her own, is not easily provoked, thinketh no evil... (1 Corinthians 13:5, KJV)

Jesus gave a clear example of this when He did exactly what God wanted Israel to do, loving the Lord with all His heart and soul, following Him, fearing Him, keeping His commandments, obeying His voice, and serving and cleaving to Him.

It's all about Him! We are honoured to have received the invitation to follow Him.

Day Forty-Seven

CLEANLINESS BRINGS SAFETY

Get out! Get out and leave your captivity, where everything you touch is unclean. Get out of there and purify yourselves, you who carry home the sacred objects of the Lord. You will not leave in a hurry, running for your lives. For the Lord will go ahead of you; yes, the God of Israel will protect you from behind. (Isaiah 52:11–12, NLT)

WHEN WE HEAR the call to follow Jesus, we can get it mixed up with the call we heard when we first came to Jesus. There was only one way we could come to him, and it was a come-as-you-are type of call. We made the decision to come to Him while we were broken, unclean, and guilty. It was the only way we could meet Him.

Whenever we're in captivity to ourselves, we're unable to be clean because there is nothing clean in our captivity. There's no difference between a self-serving criminal and a self-absorbed pastor; both are unable to be clean because they're in captivity, serving only themselves. Unfortunately, everything they touch is unclean.

Thankfully, no matter how unclean we are we can come to Jesus, like the leper:

> And, behold, there came a leper and worshipped him, saying, Lord, if thou wilt, thou canst make me clean. And Jesus put forth his hand, and touched him, saying, I will; be thou clean. And immediately his leprosy was cleansed. (Matthew 8:2, KJV)

The touch of Jesus changes everything. In a moment, we go from unclean to clean, simply by His touch. Now we can experience the joy of God opening the doors ahead of us and protecting our backside.

I always felt good after finishing a day of work in the shop. But it was difficult going into the house if I still had greasy hands, because I left a mark on everything I touched. I had to be careful with my hands!

This all changed though after showering and changing clothes. Then I could touch anything and not leave a dirty mark. I felt safe.

There is great freedom when I'm clean. I will treasure the protecting presence of God and stay clean as I follow Him.

Day Forty-Eight

THE BENEFITS OF PURITY

In a wealthy home some utensils are made of gold and silver, and some are made of wood and clay. The expensive utensils are used for special occasions, and the cheap ones are for everyday use. If you keep yourself pure, you will be a special utensil for honorable use. Your life will be clean, and you will be ready for the Master to use you for every good work.

Run from anything that stimulates youthful lusts. Instead, pursue righteous living, faithfulness, love, and peace. Enjoy the companionship of those who call on the Lord with pure hearts. (2 Timothy 2:20–22, NLT)

WHEN WE HAVE no purpose in life and have nothing to do, we can view ourselves as having very little, or even no value. This conclusion isn't necessarily true. As Paul told Timothy, the value is in the quality of the vessel. You can drink water from a clay cup just like you can from a gold cup. The water quenches your thirst no matter what.

But there is a problem if the cup is dirty. Then it can contaminate the water you're drinking. So when we have a choice, we normally choose the cleanest-looking cup and avoid the dirty one.

It is true, though, that God can use dirty things like the River Jordon, where the leper Naaman had to dip himself seven times to get his healing. His heart's desire was to use clean people, to prevent them from contaminating other people's lives. Dirty shoes spread dirt on the floor just like dirty hands leave dirt on everything they touch. A dirty heart leaves dirt on every action it motivates.

Our goal should be more than just becoming fancy vessels that get used on special occasions. That would be nothing more than an expression of external religion, an expression of beauty without godly substance.

We are challenged to keep ourselves pure. Purity is the condition that gets us on the shelf where the Master's hand goes when He wants a special utensil for honourable use. It's on this shelf that we remain ready for Him to use us for every good work. None of this work will be contaminated by any unclean thing in our lives, because we are clean.

> Blessed are the pure in heart: for they shall see God.
> (Matthew 5:8, KJV)

The benefits of a clean heart open my eyes to see God, allowing me to enjoy the companionship of others who are following with a clean heart.

Day Forty-Nine

LET US RETURN

Come, and let us return unto the Lord: for he hath torn, and he will heal us; he hath smitten, and he will bind us up. After two days will he revive us: in the third day he will raise us up, and we shall live in his sight. Then shall we know, if we follow on to know the Lord: his going forth is prepared as the morning; and he shall come unto us as the rain, as the latter and former rain unto the earth. (Hosea 6:1–3, KJV)

THE CHILDREN OF Israel were in big trouble with God. They had become so enamoured of the power of the nations around them that they tried to become like them. It was a sad situation, because they no longer remembered the great men who had once led them in the ways of God.

Their drift away from the path of God was slow but steady. They forgot all the great things they had once treasured of God. Soon there was no longer any truth, mercy, or knowledge of God in their lives.

This is why God declared in Hosea 4:1 that He had a controversy with Israel. They understood well what He meant. He was declaring a contest to show who was the greatest. It would be clearly proven!

And there was no question as to who would win this contest. The God they had minimized and desired to replace was the strongest, not to mention he controlled their condition and could overcome them in a moment.

We can too easily be like them today, drifting into the same mentality. The more we maximize ourselves and try to mimic the dynamic of others, we naturally begin to see God as something less than He is. Soon after, our hunger to follow Him no longer motivates us and we choose paths with disastrous destinations.

This is extremely difficult, yet it's where God does His work of mending us, wrapping up our wounds, and bringing us back to life. He finishes by standing us up again so we can live in His presence.

Then, finally, we get to know Him well and see Him with our own eyes, but only if we stay on the path and keep our eyes on Him. By His grace, we can!

Day Fifty

DRAW ME

The song of songs, which is Solomon's. Let him kiss
me with the kisses of his mouth: for thy love is better
than wine. Because of the savour of thy good oint-
ments thy name is as ointment poured forth, therefore do the virgins love thee. Draw me, we will run
after thee: the king hath brought me into his chambers: we will be glad and rejoice in thee, we will remember thy love more than wine: the upright love
thee. (Song of Soloman 1:1–4, KJV)

THE SHULAMITE WOMAN had an amazing love for her king. This
story presents a perfect picture of the true love we experience for
our King, Jesus. It's not a fairy tale; it's the clearest expression of the
greatest possible kind of love.

When someone is repulsive to you, the last thing you want is for
them to kiss you on the lips! However, the same experience is pleasant in the presence of love.

In biblical times, kissing had another purpose. It was used to
seal or renew a covenant between two people who trusted each other. It was serious business when a covenant was sealed with a kiss.

The Shulamite woman eagerly anticipated the time when the
king would seal their covenant of love with the kiss of his mouth.
She knew that his love was the most powerfully attractive force
anyone could experience. It would draw her to him and cause her
to run after him her whole life. She would *run*, implying that every
part of her being would participate in the effort of chasing after the
one she loved.

It's an amazing experience to know the touch of the Lord's hand, but the kiss of His mouth brings us into His chambers where we become acquainted with Him. The touch of His hand awakens us to His gift, but the touch of His lips overwhelms us with His love. Nothing will stop us from running after Him.

Don't be afraid of the intimate touch of God. It brings freedom and clarity to everything you see and will help you stay on the path, following Him.

Day Fifty-One
SEE HIM AS HE IS

Who hath believed our report? and to whom is the arm of the Lord revealed? For he shall grow up before him as a tender plant, and as a root out of a dry ground: he hath no form nor comeliness; and when we shall see him, there is no beauty that we should desire him. (Isaiah 53:1–2, KJV)

TRUTHFUL INFORMATION CAN help us navigate life. But I must have knowledge to understand and apply that truth appropriately.

In today's passage, Isaiah begins by asking two different and very important questions. Who believes the information we gave? And who has seen the naked, uncovered arm of the Lord as it really is? Seeing the naked, uncovered arm of the Lord will have a totally different effect on your life than simply believing some information about Him, even when that information is perfectly accurate.

A person could spend many hours reading books and gathering information about flying an airplane and understand every sequence of the landing process. But until you've been trained to coordinate your hand on the yoke and feet on the pedals, fixing your eyes on the runway, none of this information can produce a successful landing.

Few people would trust a pilot to fly them to a destination if that pilot didn't have firsthand experience. Isaiah wanted to point out that some would only gather information about the One who was to come, while others would experience His reality.

Many religious leaders had only learned about His coming informationally, and so they couldn't recognize Him. Then there were the shepherds and wise men who immediately recognized Him as the King even though He was lying in a feeding trough for sheep.

Since I want to keep following Him and stay on the path, I must see and experience His naked, uncovered arm. To whom is the arm of the Lord revealed? Will it be me?

Day Fifty-Two

SEE THE BEAUTY

For he shall grow up before him as a tender plant, and as a root out of a dry ground: he hath no form nor comeliness; and when we shall see him, there is no beauty that we should desire him. He is despised and rejected of men; a man of sorrows, and acquainted with grief: and we hid as it were our faces from him; he was despised, and we esteemed him not. Surely he hath borne our griefs, and carried our sorrows: yet we did esteem him stricken, smitten of God, and afflicted. (Isaiah 53:2–4, KJV)

THERE WERE MANY prophecies about what Jesus would be like when He came. There were also prophecies regarding how people would view and relate to Him. Amazingly, the way many people viewed Him was totally different from the way He really was.

My wife loves working with plants in the greenhouse and garden, so every spring we get to see the beautiful, tender plants change the landscape from dry, barren soil to flourishing green plants. When we don't see plants soon enough, we just dig a bit and soon notice the tender roots working their way into the soil. This was especially noticeable in the northern Yukon after a long cold winter when spring came very fast. Everyone who came by our house in the spring noticed the plants coming up!

How could it be then that when Jesus came as a tender plant, we concluded there was nothing delightful to be seen? We saw no beauty in the most graphic picture of love that could ever be shown.

That's why He is still despised and rejected today, just like He was despised during His physical life on the earth.

The painful experiences that continue to bring us grief detract from our ability to see the beauty of what God has brought us. I won't see His beauty until I experience the freedom that comes from Him taking, and carrying away, my griefs and sorrows.

It takes more than just knowing information about the actions of Jesus; I must experience those actions in my life before my eyes will be opened to His beauty. Otherwise, when I see Him, I will see no beauty and choose not to follow Him.

I easily follow the one I highly esteem but turn away from the one I despise. How do I see Jesus today?

Day Fifty-Three

THE BEAUTY OF HIS CHARACTER

But he was wounded for our transgressions, he was bruised for our iniquities: the chastisement of our peace was upon him; and with his stripes we are healed. All we like sheep have gone astray; we have turned every one to his own way; and the Lord hath laid on him the iniquity of us all. He was oppressed, and he was afflicted, yet he opened not his mouth: he is brought as a lamb to the slaughter, and as a sheep before her shearers is dumb, so he openeth not his mouth. (Isaiah 53:5–7, KJV)

YOU'LL LEARN ONE thing about sheep if you try to raise them: they'll get out of your fence and run free. The second thing is that they'll never find their way back inside the fence, even if the hole they made to get out is obvious. You have to open the gate and chase them back in.

I know this because we had sheep when I was growing up on a farm in Nebraska. To me, the sheep were extremely dumb and difficult to deal with.

In my late teens, I discovered that I was just like those sheep, always getting out but never finding my way back. When I read Isaiah 53 now, I discover that we are all like those sheep, always getting out and never finding our way back. We have a problem!

Thankfully, as always, God knows what to do and He does it perfectly. The evil inside us drove us to break outside of the restrictions that God set up to keep us safe. We had no peace, only agitation. This kind of lifestyle has consequences. It led to wounding, bruising, and chastisement. People are badly hurt, beaten to the point of collapse, and reprimanded.

It should have been me, but Jesus took that all in my place. And He didn't stop there. He took a beating that left Him black and blue so I could be healed. Now I'm not the same person I was. I am healed!

> Lead me in thy truth, and teach me: for thou art the
> God of my salvation; on thee do I wait all the day.
> (Psalm 25:5, KJV)

David offered the perfect prayer, knowing that God would teach and lead him into the experience of truth, giving him the ability to wait for Him to open the gates.

We too must acquire that ability to wait so we can get rid of the urge to bust through the fence and go where we don't belong. I will wait, perfectly healed and perfectly content.

Day Fifty-Four

PERFECT SUBMISSION

He was oppressed, and he was afflicted, yet he opened not his mouth: he is brought as a lamb to the slaughter, and as a sheep before her shearers is dumb, so he openeth not his mouth. He was taken from prison and from judgment: and who shall declare his generation? for he was cut off out of the land of the living: for the transgression of my people was he stricken. And he made his grave with the wicked, and with the rich in his death; because he had done no violence, neither was any deceit in his mouth. (Isaiah 53:7–9, KJV)

THE QUALITY OF our character is most easily seen in the condition of our mouths—maybe even in whether it's simply open or closed.

This part of Isaiah's prophesy points to the mouth of Jesus three times. Twice we are told that He didn't open His mouth, and once we learn that there was no deceit in His mouth. The actions of Jesus proved this true.

And the chief priests accused him of many things: but he answered nothing. And Pilate asked him again, saying, Answerest thou nothing? behold how many things they witness against thee. But Jesus yet answered nothing; so that Pilate marvelled. (Mark 15:3–5, KJV)

For many years, I heard my father preach about Jesus being the perfect sacrifice, bringing us redemption. It made no sense to me. I didn't see how any of this could be true.

That is, until one day I was working in a slaughterhouse. People mostly brought in cows or pigs in to be slaughtered, but this particular Saturday someone brought in a lamb. I knew how to kill other animals, but not a lamb, so I went to talk to my boss. He gave me a simple instruction on how to kill a lamb: "Straddle it, lift its head, and cut its throat."

I was a seventeen-year-old with a bad attitude and a hard heart, so I knew this would be easy. I straddled the lamb, expecting a fight. I lifted its head. Blood ran all over my hand as I cut its throat with my knife. There was no fight, no sound, from the lamb.

My knees went weak as I remembered the words my dad had read from the pulpit: "As a lamb to the slaughter, He opened not His mouth." This powerful experience was the beginning of my encounter with God. It changed everything.

In our loud world, we easily lose the powerful testimony of silence. Unfortunately, we default to proud resistance as we declare our God-given rights. Yes, even Christians do this. We announce that our rights won't be taken from us by anyone! It seems easier to resist governmental rules than it is to quietly submit to Jesus and follow His example.

Jesus performed many powerful works, healing people, stopping storms, and walking on water. Yet during the greatest test in His life, when He could have called upon thousands of angels, He kept His mouth shut, showing us what it is to be without deceit.

God, help us discover the beauty of a closed mouth.

Day Fifty-Five

THE LORD'S PLEASURE

And he made his grave with the wicked, and with the rich in his death; because he had done no violence, neither was any deceit in his mouth. Yet it pleased the Lord to bruise him; he hath put him to grief: when thou shalt make his soul an offering for sin, he shall see his seed, he shall prolong his days, and the pleasure of the Lord shall prosper in his hand. (Isaiah 53:9–10, KJV)

SO MANY EVENTS in Jesus's life seem contradictory. In Isaiah 53, we are told that He would be condemned and killed with wicked men, yet He was buried as a highly esteemed man.

He carried all my guilt and shame even though He did nothing wrong. Nothing! He committed no violence at all, speaking not a hint of deceit.

As always, there is a reason for these contradictions.

Despite His innocence, it was God's plan for Jesus to walk this path and be condemned as a criminal. Jesus followed the plan perfectly and encouraged His listeners to do the same. He could teach it perfectly because He lived it perfectly. He could see beyond the pain of the trials. Fear didn't stop Him. He lived for the pleasure of His Father.

But rather seek ye the kingdom of God; and all these things shall be added unto you. Fear not, little flock; for it is your Father's good pleasure to give you the kingdom. (Luke 12:31–32, KJV)

The Father's pleasure must have been highly rewarding and motivating for Jesus.

In July 2000, several of my family members met in Hoonah, Alaska to go fishing for halibut. I caught a 198-pound halibut and everyone cheered and congratulated me. It felt good to be honoured that way.

But the greatest honour I received came on the following Sunday morning after I ministered at a local church. My father, who had been a pastor for forty years, came to me at the end of the service and said, "That was very good." His pleasure was visible. I felt satisfied and rewarded, not just because of the words spoken but because my father had been the one to speak them.

Our pleasure is not found in receiving a kingdom, but in knowing that it's the Father's pleasure to give it. Whatever comes along in your journey, fear not. Look for His pleasure.

Day Fifty-Six

HE WILL BE SATISFIED

He shall see of the travail of his soul, and shall be satisfied: by his knowledge shall my righteous servant justify many; for he shall bear their iniquities. Therefore will I divide him a portion with the great, and he shall divide the spoil with the strong; because he hath poured out his soul unto death: and he was numbered with the transgressors; and he bare the sin of many, and made intercession for the transgressors. (Isaiah 53:11–12, KJV)

WHAT WOULD WE be like if we were conscious of God's satisfaction with us? It was prophesied that God would be satisfied when He saw the travail of Jesus's soul. Those would be the times when Jesus was worn out, tired, tempted, and taunted by the religious crowd of His day. Jesus knew He had come to bring justification, which would require Him to carry their burdensome iniquities. He didn't just carry those iniquities to the cross, though; He carried them every time they slandered Him. God's satisfaction was with Him every day as He did what was required to bring redemption.

I wonder how often Jesus sensed His Father's satisfaction towards Him. The nights He spent alone on the mountain would have been long, but they also would have been very rewarding when He received a sense of His Father's satisfaction while walking back down to meet the disciples in the morning.

Jesus said, *"I and my Father are one"* (John 10:30, KJV) so He had to feel a good sense of satisfaction. This satisfaction came from their relationship, with each knowing that the other would faithfully carry out His responsibilities to perfectly finish the plan they had agreed to.

This is in direct opposition to those who serve themselves, totally forgetting God and finding no lasting satisfaction.

His watchmen are blind: they are all ignorant, they are all dumb dogs, they cannot bark; sleeping, lying down, loving to slumber. Yea, they are greedy dogs which can never have enough, and they are shepherds that cannot understand: they all look to their own way, every one for his gain, from his quarter. Come ye, say they, I will fetch wine, and we will fill ourselves with strong drink; and to morrow shall be as this day, and much more abundant. (Isaiah 56:10–12, KJV)

This is the opposite of the dynamic Jesus had with His Father. The relationship I have with Jesus will be clearly seen in my life. It will show satisfaction. Without it, I will strive restlessly to achieve significance.

Resting in satisfaction gives me good sleep at the end of the day.

HE GUIDES THE MEEK

The meek will he guide in judgment: and the meek will he teach his way. All the paths of the Lord are mercy and truth unto such as keep his covenant and his testimonies. (Psalm 25:9–10, KJV)

WHEN YOU TRAVEL on unfamiliar roads, it's to your advantage to use maps to guide you. Or better yet, to have someone beside you telling you where to go and what to expect around the next curve—someone who knows how to keep you informed. This helps avoid mistakes.

I've had to backtrack more than once while traveling due to missing a turn that wasn't well marked.

I don't know if David ever got lost while taking care of the sheep, but he knew something about God carefully helping them find their way back when they ventured off-course. These same ones can find help so they don't get lost. The meek and humble seem to get His attention.

How did David learn this? He went from being an unknown shepherd to a heroic giant slayer, and then he was crowned king of a nation. Even though his position in life changed dramatically, David's consistent attitude of humility cleared the way for God to bring truth and clarity to every situation he encountered on his ever-changing path.

Humility in our lives isn't connected to our status; it's connected to the condition of our hearts. There probably were proud shepherds and humble kings in David's day, but he learned that the advantage went to the humble. They had truth and clarity in everything they faced. This would be a great asset in life, whether a person was a king or shepherd.

When I made my commitment to follow my good Shepherd, there was no question in my heart as to who was greatest. He had proven Himself to be the greatest, and I had proven myself to be not so much of anything.

It's an honour when He shows me the way when I can't find it. He takes me there when I can't make it.

Day Fifty-Eight

STUMBLING BLOCKS OR LIVELY STONES?

> So then every one of us shall give account of himself to God. Let us not therefore judge one another any more: but judge this rather, that no man put a stumblingblock or an occasion to fall in his brother's way. (Romans 14:12–13, KJV)

> Though I speak with the tongues of men and of angels, and have not charity, I am become as sounding brass, or a tinkling cymbal. (1 Corinthians 13:1, KJV)

WHY DID PAUL have to write to the church in Rome and tell them not to put a stumbling block in their brothers' path? The second part is almost more concerning: "Don't set a hidden trap or snare in your brother's way."

Usually when we leave stumbling blocks and snares in our brothers' path, it happens because of something we lack rather than something we have. We wouldn't knowingly do something to make our brother fall or get trapped in something that would harm him.

These obstacles left on the path didn't get there as a result of a simple decision. They are a result of the condition of my heart and character. When my heart is clean, the influence of my life is clean; when my heart is unclean, the influence of my life is like garbage strewn on the path behind me.

I've driven on lots of northern roads. When the snow melts in spring, there's a lot of garbage in the ditches. It's distracting to try to figure out what some of the stuff is and how it got there. It's hard to ignore! The distraction of the garbage can be as deadly as the tread of a big truck's tire lying in the middle of the road.

No one purposefully put these things there. The truck tire ended up there because of a defect, and the garbage probably just flew out the back of a pickup.

The lack of love in my life can also produce a lot of garbage on the path behind me. Great and wonderful words can be spoken by almost anyone, even those who are short on love. When I live without love, my life is nothing more than an empty, hollow vessel, irritating and distracting. This kind of life is like a stumbling block in my brother's path.

When my life is motivated by love, I leave no stumbling blocks in anyone's path.

Day Fifty-Nine

WHO AM I?

> And though I have the gift of prophecy, and understand all mysteries, and all knowledge; and though I have all faith, so that I could remove mountains, and have not charity, I am nothing. And though I bestow all my goods to feed the poor, and though I give my body to be burned, and have not charity, it profiteth me nothing. (1 Corinthians 13:2–3, KJV)

BEFORE GOD OPENS up and shows us what love looks like, He makes some very clear statements about what it is not. The last thing God desires is for people to go through all the actions of walking with Him without being anywhere near Him. That is hypocrisy, or playacting.

> And we have known and believed the love that God hath to us. God is love; and he that dwelleth in love dwelleth in God, and God in him. (1 John 4:16, KJV)

When our lives are built on the foundation of knowing and experiencing the love God has for us, we have no problem living that love for the benefit of others.

One of the first things we learn about God is that He is love. This isn't an algebraic equation where if *a* equals *b*, then *b* equals *a*. The word *is* does not mean *equal to*. A more descriptive wording here would be *is consistent with*. God is consistent in His demonstration of love. Therefore, the apostle John would also use the word "dwelleth," which means to consistently stay.

If I choose to focus my energy on acquiring and perfecting a gift from God, or any natural attribute, I lose consistency in abiding in God's love. I forget that I am complete in Him and try to set up my life like I would garden equipment, making all my equipment start quickly, run smoothly, and finish the job. Everything may be working smoothly, but I'm nothing without love.

When I'm nothing, when I need significance, I dramatically give things away hoping for some recognition. But without love there is no profit.

> Be ye therefore followers of God, as dear children;
> and walk in love, as Christ also hath loved us…
> (Ephesians 5:1–2, KJV)

Follow Jesus! He gave us the perfect example.

THE MARK OF LOVE

Charity suffereth long, and is kind; charity envieth not; charity vaunteth not itself, is not puffed up... (1 Corinthians 13:4, KJV)

ON THE PATH of life, there are things that cause people to stand out. God made it that way. This is seen very well in the life of Jesus as He walked the earth, doing the will of His Father. He stood out.

The religious people weren't drawn to Him, but broken sinners soon noticed and started coming. Those who came broken and empty found what they needed in Jesus. He lived patience and kindness. There was no competition in Him, no bragging about Himself, no acting proudly. Even though He was the Son of God, He wasn't driven by an inflated ego. The love He had for His Father was His motivation.

I've been involved in mission work for many years and have noticed how differently people approach this work. The ones who most often find the blessing of God on their work are motivated by their love of Jesus. They aren't driven by an attitude of superiority to promote the culture they were born into, or to promote their religious culture. Because of this, it's easy for them to be patient and kind, even when facing huge opposition.

An excellent example of this can be seen in Bruce Olson's book *Bruchko*. In it, he tells the story of his work with the Moltilone Bari people in Columbia. I read this book many years ago but have never forgotten the attitude Bruce had. He prayed and wanted to see what Jesus would look like in the Moltilone culture. With a humble heart, he served them while enduring great difficulties.

Eventually Jesus came and lived among those people. He was seen in that culture.

> Jesus answered and said unto him, If a man love me, he will keep my words: and my Father will love him, and we will come unto him, and make our abode with him. (John 14:23, KJV)

Jesus gave no requirements to those who wanted to follow Him except to deny themselves and take up their cross. This removes everything that would get in my way as I walk, keeping the trash off the trail behind me. Then I can enjoy walking with Him in love.

A CONSISTENT EXPRESSION

Doth not behave itself unseemly, seeketh not her own, is not easily provoked, thinketh no evil; rejoiceth not in iniquity, but rejoiceth in the truth... (1 Corinthians 13:5–6, KJV)

CONSISTENCY IS A great thing to have in our character. The best athletes become irrelevant when their actions on the playing field are no longer consistent; they can no longer be trusted. Eventually, all athletes retire from their sport for one reason or another. But this should never be the case for someone on the path of Jesus, following His footsteps.

One mark for someone on this path is that they never behave unseemly or unbecoming. All actions motivated by love are becoming, very proper and tasteful. Those who aren't motivated by love seek themselves; they are easily irritated and come to wrong and hurtful conclusions about others while expecting special treatment for themselves.

But God has done the most wonderful thing for all. It changes our lives now and for eternity. While we were in our worst condition and had nothing to offer Him in return, He loved us (Romans 5:8). Now we can love, because He first loved us.

We love him, because he first loved us. (1 John 4:19, KJV)

The greatest fulfillment in life happens when we follow His example of love.

No man hath seen God at any time. If we love one another, God dwelleth in us, and his love is perfected in us. (1 John 4:12, KJV)

Can you imagine what life would be like if everyone who claimed to believe in Jesus would walk this path? The dynamic effect of love being perfected in us would change our world.

Why wait? It's available today.

Day Sixty-Two

ALL THINGS AND EVERYWHERE

Beareth [silently endure] all things, believeth [rely
on Christ in] all things, hopeth [expect] all things,
endureth [stay under] all things. (1 Corinthians
13:7, KJV)

THIS PASSAGE REALLY gets my attention because *"all things"*
doesn't leave much room for exceptions, especially when it has to
do with silently enduring everything that comes our way.

Many years ago, I had an operation on my left hand to remove a
tendon that was so scarred that I couldn't open my hand. It had been
painful for a long time. As the hospital staff prepared me for surgery,
which I would be awake for, they had me fill out a form with lots of
questions regarding my pain tolerance. I made it very clear that I
wanted no pain anymore—none! I expected they would deaden my
hand completely so I wouldn't feel anything.

Finally, they started. They sanitized my hand and inserted nee-
dles in both arms as I lay on the table. Then they put up a curtain so
I wouldn't be able to see what they were doing to my hand.

I could hear them talking as they started to work. I also felt a
slight sensation. Suspecting that they were cutting into my hand, I
asked, "What are you seeing?" That was all I remember until I woke
up and my hand was bandaged. I had endured no pain. What had I
missed? It may have been something valuable.

What is there in love that gives power for us to endure every painful trial while expecting the goodness of God to carry us through? If
I intend to journey under the influence of love, I need a greater capacity for silence. The time and energy that goes into analyzing the

details of our difficulties would be better used by patiently waiting for God to show us His way. In waiting, my eyes turn toward Him instead of the difficulty, giving me perspective in my adversity.

> Blessed is the man that endureth [stays under] temptation [adversity]: for when he is tried, he shall receive the crown of life, which the Lord hath promised to them that love him. (James 1:12, KJV)

God gives the supreme honour of life to those whose love of Him is proven by their choice to endure the painful trials of faith rather than insist on the absence of pain.

Day Sixty-Three

THE ONE WHO NEVER FAILS

Charity never faileth: but whether there be prophecies, they shall fail; whether there be tongues, they shall cease; whether there be knowledge, it shall vanish away. (1 Corinthians 13:8, KJV)

WE CAN BE assured of great security when the stuff we accumulate is expected to last long. We're confident that we'll get lots of good use from it. Manufacturers like to promote the idea that their products will last long, but none of them ever admit that the product will eventually fail, even though everyone knows it will. So we just close our eyes and hope for the best.

There are some things that we know are going to fail. This information comes from a very reliable source: God. All talk promoting knowledge of what is and is to come is impressive and admired, but it has a dramatic end. It's like a spaceship exploding in outer space, then burning up as it falls through the earth's atmosphere. The bits and pieces of ash that remain fall into the oceans and are never seen again—ever.

Since talking requires less energy and commitment than loving, that's often the first action we choose. When we then experience the high failure rate of talk and are left with almost nothing, we begin looking for something that lasts. It may take time and failure, but eventually the hunger in our hearts opens us up to the eternal influence of love. Once you know it, you won't let go of it, and it won't let go of you.

The powerful influence of love becomes known in the slightest touch. Many people were healed when Jesus touched them; others touched Jesus and were healed. While the action of touch is important, the touch didn't make the healing work. The healing was a work of love directly from the heart of Father God.

Most of my mechanic tools have broken eventually. They're no longer useful. But the love I received when I met Jesus is still fresh and new. It never fails!

Day Sixty-Four

WHEN LOVE SHOWS UP

For we know in part, and we prophesy in part. But when that which is perfect is come, then that which is in part shall be done away. (1 Corinthians 13:9–10, KJV)

DISASTROUS THINGS CAN happen when we go through life thinking we know all about what we're doing, when we only know a small part. We can feel satisfied as we learn to do more and more things over the course of our lives.

Knowledge can be a good thing, helping us to be successful, and in some cases a little knowledge can even keep us alive.

On the other hand, a lack of knowledge can get us killed. When I was having a heart attack and in very bad pain, I did nothing about it because I didn't recognize the symptoms of a heart attack. I thought that my left arm would hurt. Thankfully, I survived despite my lack of knowledge.

Unfortunately, we have two problems. We don't know what we don't know, so we can't fix it. Secondly, the knowledge we have is only a small piece of the whole, even if our knowledge is extensive. But no matter how much we know, it's a very small part of what can be known.

Paul knew this well and wrote about it.

Now as touching things offered unto idols, we know that we all have knowledge. Knowledge puffeth up, but charity edifieth. And if any man think that he knoweth any thing, he knoweth nothing yet as he

ought to know. But if any man love God, the same is
known of him. (1 Corinthians 8:1–3, KJV)

We have a dilemma! Not only is all our knowledge only a small
part of the whole, but the more we focus on it the prouder we become. It doesn't build us up; it puffs us up and takes up way too
much space in our lives.

Then God brings love, perfect and complete, changing our relationship with everything, including the knowledge we have. Our
advantage is no longer in knowing facts, but in knowing God and
Him knowing us.

The things we don't know no longer matter because we have
love which is perfect and complete.

Day Sixty-Five

TIME TO GROW UP

*When I was a child, I spake as a child, I understood as
a child, I thought as a child: but when I became a man,
I put away childish things. (1 Corinthians 13:11, KJV)*

THE CHILD IN this passage is described as an infant, or immature
Christian. The behaviour of a small child is predictable. Their whole
process of speaking, understanding, and thinking is self-centred.
These are not bad behaviours that need correction. They are normal
for a young child.

As we grow into adults, we leave the childish things behind. It's
hard to describe everything that's childish, but it's noticeable when a
grown person behaves like a child. Likewise, we've probably all seen
a small child try and act like an adult.

It's interesting to note that we don't mature by putting away
childish behaviour. Rather, childish behaviour simply gets left behind
as we grow up.

A young child's way of walking is often unbalanced. They focus
and work hard to keep their balance but still fall more often than an
adult. When my grandchildren were learning to walk and lost their
balance, there were sometimes tears. Other times they even hit their
head when they fell.

But as an adult, I rarely if ever spend time thinking about my balance. When an adult walks unsteadily, we take notice. Something is
wrong.

As followers of Jesus, the mature will follow differently than
those who are just beginning to walk. Paul described it clearly to the
Ephesians:

That we henceforth be no more children, tossed to and fro, and carried about with every wind of doctrine, by the sleight of men, and cunning craftiness, whereby they lie in wait to deceive; but speaking the truth in love, may grow up into him in all things, which is the head, even Christ... (Ephesians 4:14–15, KJV)

It's important to note that we don't mature spiritually by getting props to keep us from getting tossed about. It's not about building good wind shelters to prevent the wind from carrying us away. Neither is it about gaining more knowledge so we won't be deceived by manipulative people. The one who is no longer a child has entered into a more mature relationship with Christ, stabilized by His love.

Living on the path of love eliminates our childish tendencies and takes us further into the fullness of Christ.

NOW AND THEN

For now we see through a glass, darkly; but then face to face: now I know in part; but then shall I know even as also I am known. And now abideth faith, hope, charity, these three; but the greatest of these is charity. (1 Corinthians 13:12–13, KJV)

THERE ARE THREE parts of life that affect us: the past, present, and future.

The past, which at one time was the present, is over because it's behind us. As with taking off in an airplane, there is a simple rule to remember: "There is no value in the runway behind you." So when I used to take off, I never wasted any part of the runway. When it was very short, I pushed the tail of the airplane right up against the trees behind me; in the winter, I pushed right up against snowbanks. That way, every foot of the runway was available ahead of me.

Once the present becomes the past, you can't go back and utilize it. While there may be good lessons to be learned from the past, it can also be wasted and lost.

> While it is said, To day if ye will hear his voice, harden not your hearts, as in the provocation. (Hebrews 3:15, KJV)

This statement is made three times in the book of Hebrews. It's a great reminder of what the children of Israel did on their journey through the wilderness. It is so important for us to keep our hearts soft in the present, otherwise they become hard and stubborn.

The present, which Paul calls "now," has great value. What we do today will greatly impact tomorrow, also called "then."

In the same way, my future is greatly impacted by what I do today, just like today has been impacted by all my yesterdays. This was an important point in Paul's message to the Corinthian church.

The lesson is clear: we must focus on the here and now, even though it's like looking through very dark glasses, if we ever intend to see God face to face. We must be aware of Him now, even though it's only a small part of our lives, if we intend to know Him as completely as He knows us.

> Seek ye the Lord while he may be found, call ye upon him while he is near… (Isaiah 55:6, KJV)

There is one more great blessing of today. It is only *now* that we can expect faith, hope, and love to be always present. These aren't accessible in the past, nor are they promised for the future. They are current and will remain current.

Don't waste your *now* on things that will have no value *then*.

IF GOD BE GOD

And Elijah came unto all the people, and said, How
long halt ye between two opinions? if the Lord be
God, follow him: but if Baal, then follow him. And
the people answered him not a word. (1 Kings
18:21, KJV)

HOW WAS IT possible for the children of Israel to get confused
about who their God was? They were reminded of their history in so
many ways as they celebrated their deliverance from Egypt. Yet they
seemed to lose their vital connection to the reality of the One who
had delivered them and given them the Promised Land.

It is obvious they had some knowledge of God because they
feared and revered Him. But they didn't serve Him. Instead they
served the images they had carved out of wood and stone, which
represented the things that had value to them. These images they
lived for had a heavy pull on their hearts.

They had some respect for God, but it wasn't enough to motivate them to serve Him. And the Israelites' children then followed the
example of their fathers.

So these nations feared the Lord, and served their
graven images, both their children, and their children's children: as did their fathers, so do they unto
this day. (2 Kings 17:41, KJV)

The day finally came when the prophet Elijah confronted the
people and forced them to make a decision. They would have to

identify the one true God and follow Him. It would mean no longer serving the idols of Baal that demanded their service.

This upended their lives. Their minds and hearts were so confused that at first they didn't have a reply for Elijah.

After years of going back and forth between God and Baal, never anchored in either, their chaos must have been overpowering. They were about to see God for themselves. Then they would make their choice.

Today I make my choice. My decision will determine who I serve today: the true God or the gods of this world that scream for my attention.

> Know ye that the Lord he is God: it is he that hath
> made us, and not we ourselves; we are his people,
> and the sheep of his pasture. (Psalm 100:3, KJV)

Day Sixty-Eight

THE DELIGHT OF THE BLESSED

Blessed is the man that walketh not in the counsel of the ungodly, nor standeth in the way of sinners, nor sitteth in the seat of the scornful. But his delight is in the law of the Lord; and in his law doth he meditate day and night. (Psalm 1:1–2, KJV)

WHY WOULD ANYONE live according to the advice of those who are known to be ungodly, or those who stand in solidarity with lawbreakers, or those who scoff at truth? It's obvious that something was missing and needed correction in the lives of the Israelites.

I need to know why the man mentioned in Psalm 1 was blessed. Is it because he followed some rules and didn't do certain things, or did he not do these things for the simple reason that he was blessed?

A blessed man doesn't get that way by strictly following rules. This doesn't mean that rules aren't important, though; they can save your life. While they have a purpose, they are not the end of the matter. They are meant to show us our need for justification by faith, which can only be found in Christ. When we find that kind of relationship, we are guided into maturity rather than following rules that are meant to restrict our external behaviour.

Wherefore the law was our schoolmaster to bring us unto Christ, that we might be justified by faith. But after that faith is come, we are no longer under a schoolmaster. (Galatians 3:24–25, KJV)

The heart of this blessed man in the Psalms was demonstrated in how he lived. He found great pleasure in the law because of His relationship with the One who taught him.

> Thou wilt shew me the path of life: in thy presence is fulness of joy; at thy right hand there are pleasures for evermore. (Psalm 16:11, KJV)

When I identify my most valuable pleasure, it will open my eyes to the path I'm on, as well as its destination. David got it right! His most valuable pleasure was the fullness of joy he found in the presence of God. These pleasures can be enjoyed both now and in the life to come.

Day Sixty-Nine

TRANSPLANTED BY RIVERS

And he shall be like a tree planted by the rivers of
water, that bringeth forth his fruit in his season; his
leaf also shall not wither; and whatsoever he doeth
shall prosper. (Psalm 1:3, KJV)

MY WIFE WORKS in a greenhouse every spring. At times I've
watched her work. It looks violent! The plants are pulled out of small
trays and shoved into the soft soil of bigger pots. There doesn't
appear to be much tenderness in the process, but somehow the
plants all flourish.

I've also transplanted fifteen-foot spruce trees. One needs some
pretty heavy equipment to cut the soil around the roots and lift it up
out of the hole. Then the tree gets hauled to the new location where a
hole has already been prepared for it. The tree is shaken a lot before
its roots are set back in the soil. The branches can get a bit droopy
before the roots start taking water again. That process can happen
quickly with some trees while others take a long while before they
start to look healthy again.

When David talks about the blessed man in Psalm 1, he says
that he will be like a tree planted by rivers of water. Actually, *planted* isn't the correct word. The original meaning of the word here
is "transplanted," an interesting but sometimes violent process.
Whether transplanting a small tomato plant or fifteen-foot tree, the
plant inevitably has to recover from a shock.

The blessed man gets transplanted close to rivers of water, indicating that its leaves won't be at risk of withering. Somehow the
shock will be minimized, allowing the fruit to appear at the right time.

Everything about this blessed transplanted man prospers. He continues to delight himself in the way of the Lord, even in the midst of the process.

Having a predictable life, with day-to-day routines that never change, makes us feel secure. God's intention for us goes beyond that. We aren't going to just *feel* secure; we will *be* secure. He intends for us to be transplanted by the rivers instead of remaining securely rooted in small pots in a greenhouse.

Embrace the transplanting process.

Day Seventy

THE LORD KNOWS THE WAY

> The ungodly are not so: but are like the chaff which the wind driveth away. Therefore the ungodly shall not stand in the judgment, nor sinners in the congregation of the righteous. For the Lord knoweth the way of the righteous: but the way of the ungodly shall perish. (Psalm 1:4–6, KJV)

THE UNGODLY MAN of Psalm 1 is opposite in every way to the blessed man. The blessed man prospers in all he does. His leaf doesn't wither at all. However, the ungodly man is like chaff in every way.

While growing up in Nebraska, my dad raised a lot of corn. At that time, almost everyone used corn pickers. The corn was stored on the cob. Later, my uncle would use a corn-sheller. All the cobs would be piled in one truck and the kernels of corn in another. It was always a dusty, dirty job as the chaff blew around where we worked. The chaff was itchy, dirty, and irritating, having no value.

People who live without any connection to God sometimes seem to have successful lives. However, they live with no respect for God or eternal matters. Their every decision is based on what's best for themselves. Yet they portray security while the blessed man gets uprooted and doesn't seem to have any say in the matter. His delight is in the Lord, not in the security of the present.

The reality is that the ungodly man is chaff, blown away easily by a little breeze. He has no anchor, no root, and no life. He has no ability to stand in judgment or stand with the righteous on the path of life.

The greatest security is found in the man who delights himself in the Lord. The Lord not only knows him; He also knows the path the righteous man is on. He knows the path in an intellectual way, true, but He is also intimately involved with the blessed man as he walks.

You may feel insecure as God takes you through the transplanting process, but let Him keep you in His hand as He takes you to the rivers of water. Stay with Him. The other option is to become like chaff.

Day Seventy-One

ON GUARD

I said, I will take heed [be on guard] to my ways, that I sin not with my tongue: I will keep my mouth with a bridle, while the wicked is before me. I was dumb with silence, I held my peace, even from good; and my sorrow was stirred. My heart was hot within me, while I was musing the fire burned: then spake I with my tongue, Lord, make me to know mine end, and the measure of my days, what it is: that I may know how frail I am. (Psalm 39:1–4, KJV)

WHEN I WAS in high school, I took a class on driver training. Its main purpose was to teach students how to drive a car. Most of us were living on farms and had basically grown up driving tractors and pickups, starting when we were about ten years old. By the time we were sixteen, we could safely drive almost anything, either on the farm or on the road, when needed. The course seemed pretty useless—that is, until we learned that we'd get a pretty significant discount on vehicle insurance if we took the course.

So I signed up.

The instructor was very good and taught us well. We soon learned there was a great difference between driving alone in a field and driving in town. While we wouldn't come upon other vehicles in the field, they would always be within a few feet of us in town—and we'd know nothing about the other people driving these cars.

We learned about defensive driving, a new concept for us. The instructor stressed the need to always obey the law while staying alert for other drivers who might disregard the law. These drivers were unsafe and very irritating. Defensive driving would keep us safe.

In the Bible, David writes that he would guard his ways, especially what he did with his tongue and mouth, while in the presence of the ungodly, those who lived without any guidance or godly standard. These people's conduct could be like those driving around town with no regard for the law. They aren't safe and it's easy to make unkind and judgmental remarks about them.

While David remained silent, something was happening in his heart. He wanted to know the end of the road he was on, no longer focused on those who lived without restraint. He also wanted to learn about how frail and empty he was. During the intense struggle to keep his mouth shut, refraining from the judgment of others, he became aware of his own needs.

Declare, like David, *"I will take heed."*

Day Seventy-Two

A SERVANT KNOWS

James, a servant of God and of the Lord Jesus Christ, to the twelve tribes which are scattered abroad, greeting. My brethren, count it all joy when ye fall into divers temptations; knowing this, that the trying of your faith worketh patience. But let patience have her perfect work, that ye may be perfect and entire, wanting nothing. (James 1:1–4, KJV)

JAMES CALLED HIMSELF a servant, but a more descriptive word would be *slave*. James clearly declared who he was enslaved to. Without question, he was absolutely a slave to God and the Lord Jesus Christ. This defined who he was and how he handled every situation.

Slaves were the lowest-class members of society. People didn't normally go to them for advice, especially on how to live successfully. But James knew how to live and told the twelve tribes of Israel how they could live to perfect satisfaction; it would only happen if they joyfully embraced their difficulties, recognizing that those difficulties had value for them.

This kind of lesson is only learned by experience.

That logic runs contrary to people who appear successful in our current generation. It's easy to understand. Success looks different for those who are slaves to God. A slave cheerfully goes through unexpected troubles knowing that these experiences have value, while others do everything possible to avoid trouble and eliminate those who cause it.

It's not the trouble itself that directly benefits the slave. The trouble gives them an opportunity to discover faith and operate in it. Their faith is tested in unexpected difficulties. This brings out a person's patient character. Patience is the consistent, hopeful expectation of good things. When that becomes part of who we are, and expresses itself in our lives, we will go through life without limits or lack.

Don't let difficulties derail you from following God. Find your faith and let it be tested. The process will amaze you and you'll never be the same.

Day Seventy-Three

GAIN WISDOM FOR THE JOURNEY

If any of you lack wisdom, let him ask of God, that giveth to all men liberally, and upbraideth not; and it shall be given him. But let him ask in faith, nothing wavering. For he that wavereth is like a wave of the sea driven with the wind and tossed. For let not that man think that he shall receive any thing of the Lord. (James 1:5–7, KJV)

I DON'T KNOW why James starts by writing *"If any of you lack wisdom..."* Looking at our religious culture in North America today, to me it would seem more relevant to say something like "Since we all lack wisdom..." He probably had more wisdom than me, so his words were more gracious.

But I do wonder how many people have read this and are aware of their lack of wisdom.

There are two simple ways for us to become aware of our lack of wisdom.

The first is by recognizing that we have just enough wisdom to make us aware of our lack. The other is by behaving in ways that betray our lack. The most obvious revealing behaviour is talking too much, failing to control our tongues, and failing to listen.

No matter how I become aware of my lack, God has a way of giving me a full supply of wisdom.

The answer is this: in simple faith, ask God for it. How, when, and where He does it isn't described in the Bible, although we're told we will receive a full amount. We shouldn't waver in this process. This isn't just about our faith; it's about continually committing ourselves to the process of growing in wisdom. When this happens, it will be noticeable!

For wisdom to grow, I can't be intense one day and then casual the next. I can't let the pressure of the day change my desire for the things that are important to God. My vacillation will disconnect me from the storehouse from which God supplies what we lack.

When we are full of wisdom, our lives are the truest expression of following Jesus. I will know how to open my ears and close my mouth.

Day Seventy-Four

THE PLACE FOR GENTLENESS

My dear brothers and sisters, always be willing to listen and slow to speak. Do not become angry easily, because anger will not help you live the right kind of life God wants. So put out of your life every evil thing and every kind of wrong. Then in gentleness accept God's teaching that is planted in your hearts, which can save you. (James 1:19–21, NCV)

MY ACTIONS POINT to the condition of my heart. Typically, someone who's easily angered is also quick to speak and has a hard time listening to others. If they won't listen to others, they probably won't listen to God either. This doesn't mean that they'll be compelled to agree with what others say, but they must be willing to respectfully listen, which involves more than just keeping their mouth shut.

Self-discipline helps with this process, but the biggest factor is the gentleness in one's heart.

Certain behaviours help me continue serving the Lord, and others distract me. Once I choose the action, the consequence is already set.

Some actions are easier to change than others, but they're all connected to something in life, rooted in the heart. That's why the servant James tells us to sort out every evil and wrong thing in our lives. It's very much like weeding a garden, getting out every weed without leaving even the tiniest root behind. It's also like paying close attention to the perimeter of the yard; quack grass can creep in and slowly shrink the garden, reducing its capacity to produce valuable crops.

This is a metaphor for life. The invaluable things must be removed so the valuable ones can flourish.

Now that the unclean things are out of my life, gentleness finds a place and opens the door of my heart to God, as well as those around me. This is the only condition in which the truth of God can take root and grow in my life. His provision brings me to a safe place and transforms me into a clean, safe person for others to be around.

> And she shall bring forth a son, and thou shalt call his name Jesus: for he shall save his people from their sins. (Mathew 1:21, KJV)

Jesus didn't just come to save us from the consequences of our sin; He came to save us from our sins. Gentleness opens our hearts to truth and changes our lives.

Day Seventy-Five

ACTION REQUIRED

Do what God's teaching says; when you only listen and do nothing, you are fooling yourselves. Those who hear God's teaching and do nothing are like people who look at themselves in a mirror. They see their faces and then go away and quickly forget what they looked like. But the truly happy people are those who carefully study God's perfect law that makes people free, and they continue to study it. They do not forget what they heard, but they obey what God's teaching says. Those who do this will be made happy. (James 1:22–25, NCV)

MIRRORS CAN BE valuable, even though what you see in a mirror is only a reversed image of reality. The mirror doesn't decide whether something is good or bad; it just reflects it.

When I look in a mirror and see dirt on my face, I don't wash the mirror. I wash my face. But I can also simply walk away from the mirror to avoid seeing the dirt. The dirt hasn't been cleaned away, but I don't see or remember it anymore.

It's sad, but sometimes the easiest way to live is to ignore the dirt—although if we do, we're just fooling ourselves.

The happiest people are those who can honestly see who they are in the mirror and deal with every blemish. On the other hand, the most unhappy people see themselves in the mirror and successfully forget what they saw. They don't want to face it because it doesn't match the image they have of themselves.

While I follow the Lord on His path, I need to act—that is, unless I choose to deceive myself, thinking I'm following when I'm not. God has a perfect law: the gospel. But the people who study it are different. It's like someone bending over to closely examine something, letting nothing distract them. This kind of study is intense, and so are the results. When a person studies with that kind of focus, it's not easy to put it aside and forget it afterward.

My hunger for the gospel will compel me to carefully learn more about it and ensure there's a way to show it in my own life. When we do, we'll be extremely happy with what God does in our lives.

BE REAL

If any man among you seem to be religious, and bridleth not his tongue, but deceiveth his own heart, this man's religion is vain. Pure religion and undefiled before God and the Father is this, To visit the fatherless and widows in their affliction, and to keep himself unspotted from the world. (James 1:26–27, KJV)

GOD MADE US exactly as He knew we needed to be. Every part was made perfectly and placed in the perfect location. Then, when God finished, He concluded that we were *"very good"* (Genesis 1:31). He liked us just the way we were.

Interestingly, our mouth is out front and our ears are off to the side! This seems to imply that the problem isn't the mouth or its location. Neither is it the ears or their location. The real issue that affects us is the heart.

Keep thy heart with all diligence; for out of it are the issues of life. Put away from thee a froward mouth, and perverse lips put far from thee. (Proverbs 4:23–24, KJV)

The mouth of the righteous speaketh wisdom, and his tongue talketh of judgment. The law of his God is in his heart; none of his steps shall slide. (Psalm 37:30–31, KJV)

My religion—in other words, my lived experience of seeing God—will always be seen in how I live. When I'm following the Lord, as a slave with my whole heart, the expression will be pure and undefiled. But if the expression of how I see God is vain, or an empty idol, it will be the result of me having deceived my own heart. This deceived heart takes me from willingly serving God and others to expecting Him and others to serve me; I see myself as the greatest one.

The disciples of Jesus had a problem with this as well. Can you imagine being in the presence of Jesus and asking, *"Who is the greatest in the kingdom of heaven?"* (Matthew 18:1, KJV) Their eyes were so fixed on themselves that they couldn't consider Jesus. He showed them who was the greatest by putting the spotlight on a child, not Himself.

When my heart is connected to the right person, my feet stay connected to the right path.

Day Seventy-Seven

OF ONE MIND

Finally, be ye all of one mind... (1 Peter 3:8, KJV)

Now the God of patience and consolation grant you to be likeminded one toward another according to Christ Jesus: that ye may with one mind and one mouth glorify God, even the Father of our Lord Jesus Christ. (Romans 15:5–6, KJV)

WHEN GOD CALLS us to be of one mind together, He isn't telling us all to think the same thing, exactly the same way. This is what cults are like and God has no desire for His followers to create cults.

Being of one mind is beautiful. It's like music being sung in perfect harmony. Some may sing very high notes and others low notes. Still others will sing somewhere in between. The beauty of it compels someone to listen.

The legalistic cultish mindset demands that we all rigidly chant the same words with the same monotonous sound. There is no life or beauty in that kind of oneness because God gets no glory.

We all start life in the same condition, making the same dead sound without any beauty. Then God changed everything and made us alive, giving us the ability to harmonize with others.

And you hath he quickened, who were dead in trespasses and sins... (Ephesians 2:1, KJV)

Thankfully, God is patient and consistently helps us learn to harmonize instead of drowning each other out. He does more than show us the notes and teach us how to make the right sounds. Harmony requires us to listen to the other singers as well as learn our own parts.

> Fulfil ye my joy, that ye be likeminded, having the same love, being of one accord, of one mind. Let nothing be done through strife or vainglory; but in lowliness of mind let each esteem other better than themselves. Look not every man on his own things, but every man also on the things of others. Let this mind be in you, which was also in Christ Jesus... (Philippians 2:2–5, KJV)

My voice will never be in harmony with my others if my ears won't listen to their voices. God is the perfect instructor. He will teach us how to do it.

Day Seventy-Eight

IDENTIFY WITH OTHERS

...having compassion one of another... (1 Peter 3:8, KJV)

But a certain Samaritan, as he journeyed, came where he was: and when he saw him, he had compassion on him, and went to him, and bound up his wounds, pouring in oil and wine, and set him on his own beast, and brought him to an inn, and took care of him. (Luke 10:33–34, KJV)

COMPASSION IS POWERFULLY motivating. When it isn't present in my life, I walk past people who are hurting and hardly notice them. I fail to identify with them or their condition. I feel superior in my attitude and actions.

However, when compassion is in my heart, I have the ability to identify with those who are hurting. That compassion moves me to action.

Compassion is seen in the story of the Samaritan man who encountered someone lying alongside the road. This wounded man had been beaten and it wasn't a pretty sight. Others had seen him and done nothing; they just walked on by, not wanting to get too close.

But compassion motivated the Samaritan. As soon as he saw the beaten man, he went to him! When he got there, he immediately began to minister to him in a way that began to change his condition.

As a follower of Jesus, I must be like that Samaritan man, driven to go to the hurting because of the compassion in my heart. Sometimes Christians think that God wants them to build ministries that are so attractive that hurting people come to them. The desire is for a come-and-see kind of ministry. That's probably okay.

But a person likely can't establish a come-and-see ministry until they've proven themselves able to engage in go-and-do ministry. Why? Because compassion in the heart moves a person to seek out the hurting. The come-and-see style of ministry is often more of a come-and-see-me ministry, lacking compassion.

> Then the lord of that servant was moved with com-
> passion, and loosed him, and forgave him the debt.
> (Matthew 18:27, KJV)

Yes, compassion will cost you something. In fact, it may cost you everything.

Day Seventy-Nine

THE GOSPEL MADE VISIBLE

...love as brethren... (1 Peter 3:8, KJV)

And [add] to godliness brotherly kindness; and to brotherly kindness charity. For if these things be in you, and abound, they make you that ye shall neither be barren nor unfruitful in the knowledge of our Lord Jesus Christ. But he that lacketh these things is blind, and cannot see afar off, and hath forgotten that he was purged from his old sins. (2 Peter 1:7–9, KJV)

Seeing ye have purified your souls in obeying the truth through the Spirit unto unfeigned love of the brethren, see that ye love one another with a pure heart fervently... (1 Peter 1:22, KJV)

LOVE CANNOT BE hidden. It leaves tracks, like footprints in deep snow. Likewise, when love is absent it's very obvious.

Why would love be absent? I must answer this question if I want to resolve the emptiness in my relationship with others. I can only fake it so long.

I've heard people say that while we are commanded to love each other, we aren't told that we have to *like* them. But that sounds like an impossible way for me to relate to others while still claiming to love them in the sense Peter wrote about. When I "love" in that manner, something is lacking in the relationship—and the fault doesn't lie in the other. Whatever is missing, it's missing in me.

In today's verses, Peter used the words *purged*, *purified*, and *pure*, indicating the value of cleanness.

For several years I did a lot of repairs on damaged RVs. Many of them had materials that had been glued together. I would cut out the damaged area and rebuild it with new material, then reattach it with glue. If the repair was going to remain together after the RV was driven along rough roads, all the joints had to be perfectly clean before they were joined. If they weren't clean, they would separate after just a few miles. I always had to take great care and focus to prepare for the bonding, but it was worth it to keep the RV together.

That's really what life is about. I could have faked the repair and made a nice external finish. The RV repair would have been fast and impressive when the owner drove it away from my shop, but it never would have survived the bumps on the road ahead. The uncleanness in the repair would soon be discovered.

However, the proof of a clean repair would be proven over a long period of successful travel.

> Be kindly affectioned one to another with brotherly love; in honour preferring one another... (Romans 12:9, KJV)

When my life is clean, the continued kindness expressed in my life is visible proof of the gospel in operation.

Day Eighty

COMPASSIONATE AND HUMBLE

...be pitiful, be courteous... (1 Peter 3:8, KJV)

Behold, we count them happy which endure. Ye have heard of the patience of Job, and have seen the end of the Lord; that the Lord is very pitiful, and of tender mercy. (James 5:11, KJV)

WHAT DOES IT look like when someone is pitiful? Language evolves over time and words slowly take on new meanings. Different cultures may even use the same word in a different way.

Since we're told to be pitiful on our journey as servants of the Lord, it's important for us to know whether we actually are that way. We know it was important for Jesus because James wrote about seeing *"the end of the Lord"*—or literally, the goal of the Lord. If His goal was to be "very pitiful" and a picture of "tender mercy," those traits must have had great value for Him.

It's important to have goals. Paul said, *"I press toward the mark..."* (Philippians 3:14), which is a good indication that he had a very clear goal. If you don't have a goal, be careful; you'll probably reach it, like many others. And it'll be nothing at all.

Think of how differently our lives, churches, and nations would be if we all had the goal of being pitiful, which is defined as compassionate. James said that the Lord is *very* compassionate. He reached His goal. That aspect of His character is very obvious when you read in the gospels how many times Jesus was moved by compassion to help others. Compassion overpowers critical attitudes and harsh judgments, which cause division.

Once compassion becomes part of our lives, the next step isn't hard. Peter told us to be courteous—in other words, to be humble. Having a low estimate of one's own importance, which is what it means to be humble, opens the door to obedience. If I'm having a hard time obediently serving the Lord and others, it may have something to do with the lack of humility in my life.

Jesus had an extremely important place in God's plan for us. Jesus had a job to do that would affect the eternal destiny of all humanity, yet He humbled himself and obeyed. This is the perfect example of humility and obedience going hand in hand.

> But made himself of no reputation, and took upon him the form of a servant, and was made in the likeness of men: and being found in fashion as a man, he humbled himself, and became obedient unto death, even the death of the cross. Wherefore God also hath highly exalted him, and given him a name which is above every name... (Philippians 2:7–9, KJV)

God was well pleased with the way His Son lived His life and related to others. For this reason, God highly exalted Him and gave Him a name above any other. The character of Jesus remained the same whether He was humbled or exalted. So did Paul's character. He learned how to abound without letting it change who he was (Philippians 4:11).

Successfully following Jesus requires that we be compassionate and humble. All things are possible with God, so I'll stay with Him and be changed.

Day Eighty-One

SIMPLE INSTRUCTIONS

> Not rendering evil for evil, or railing for railing: but
> contrariwise blessing; knowing that ye are thereun-
> to called, that ye should inherit a blessing. For he
> that will love life, and see good days, let him refrain
> his tongue from evil, and his lips that they speak no
> guile: let him eschew evil, and do good; let him seek
> peace, and ensue it. (1 Peter 3:9–11, KJV)

OUR HUMAN NATURE is normally predictable. When someone
wrongs us, our typical response is to do or say something to even
the score. The wrong done to us may be something said that's un-
true or worthless, or it may be something that damages our reputation or self-esteem.

It's hard to find people who are willing to sit quietly while their reputation is torn apart and lies are told about them. This kind of abuse is
stimulating and the urge to respond can be overpowering. The urge to
defend ourselves and our reputations is deeply rooted in us.

However, for true servants of the Lord Jesus, there is another
way.

When I follow Him, my attitude and actions will be different. I will
respond in other ways than I would have before following Jesus, at a
time when I was on a path with a different purpose and destiny. Now
my words and actions will show that I love life.

> Being then made free from sin, ye became the serv-
> ants of righteousness... for when ye were the serv-
> ants of sin, ye were free from righteousness... but

now being made free from sin, and become servants to God, ye have your fruit unto holiness, and
the end everlasting life. (Romans 6:18, 20, 22, KJV)

The words I speak and the actions of my life will clearly declare
that I love life as a servant who follows Jesus. May all my words and
actions be stimulated by the thoughts of my heart and be delightful
to God (Proverbs 19:14).

Day Eighty-Two

NOT AFRAID OR TROUBLED BUT HAPPY

> For the eyes of the Lord are over the righteous, and his ears are open unto their prayers: but the face of the Lord is against them that do evil. And who is he that will harm you, if ye be followers of that which is good? But and if ye suffer for righteousness' sake, happy are ye: and be not afraid of their terror, neither be troubled... (1 Peter 3:12–14, KJV)

WHEN I'M HAPPY, it's usually because nothing is giving me trouble or threatening me. Everything is peaceful and secure. Some people find happiness lying on a quiet beach on a warm sunny day with their favourite friends beside them.

The happiness Peter wrote about seems to exist on a completely different level, where trouble and fear have no influence even though they may be present. What makes this possible?

When my relationship with God is real, it impacts my life in a practical way. The information I have about Him isn't as important as my relationship with Him.

Peter knew Him well enough to state that the Lord has His eyes on those who are innocent and hears everything their hearts ask for. The King James Version uses the word *righteous*, which is easily connected to an external condition, but the definition is *innocence*, which is an internal condition of cleanness.

If I'm not clean in my heart, the only other condition in which I can exist is unclean. There is no middle ground. I am either clean or unclean.

The condition I choose will affect everything I do and impact every relationship I have, including with God. He made a way for me to be clean—if I choose it. My clean heart will be like an anchor holding me steady in every storm.

> Now ye are clean through the word which I have spoken unto you. (John 15:3, KJV)

When the Word, the divine expression of God, has its cleaning effect on me, I will be made aware of it in unusual ways. I've carried some big regrets since being saved. Memories of the bad things I did have robbed me of my peace and happiness.

Some nights, I was so troubled that I couldn't sleep, so I would get up and read my Bible. After several months, a change began to take place. The pain of these memories was diminished and my content, happy atmosphere remained. My heart was cleaned by the Word.

Happiness is normal when we follow the good path of God.

Day Eighty-Three

SERVANTS RESPOND TO WHAT'S HOLY

When Joshua was near the town of Jericho, he looked up and saw a man standing in front of him with sword in hand. Joshua went up to him and demanded, "Are you friend or foe?"

"Neither one," he replied. "I am the commander of the Lord's army."

At this, Joshua fell with his face to the ground in reverence. "I am at your command," Joshua said. "What do you want your servant to do?"

The commander of the Lord's army replied, "Take off your sandals, for the place where you are standing is holy." And Joshua did as he was told. (Joshua 5:13–15, NLT)

THIS UNEXPECTED ENCOUNTER Joshua had with a stranger started with a simple, matter-of-fact question. There was no introduction, only a question: *"Are you friend or foe?"* From Joshua's perspective, this couldn't have been a casual observer. The man was either on his side or he was an enemy.

Times were tense, as the children of Israel were ready to take over the walled city of Jericho. All its gates and doors were locked as the city prepared to defend itself. It would seem that everyone was preparing to either attack or defend the city.

Joshua didn't care who this stranger was; he only wanted to know which side he was on.

He must have been puzzled for a moment when the stranger replied that he was neither friend nor foe.

We will have many encounters with people as we serve the Lord. We easily connect with those who fight for the same things we do. But there is a distinct mark on those sent by God with clear instructions to guide us on our journeys. Such a man doesn't care about what we're for or against. He doesn't care about what we like or dislike, or about our rules of dos and don'ts. He cares for one thing only: the directives of God.

This kind of person will bring clarity to every situation we face and provide clear directions as to the path God has for us. Such an encounter removes from us the burden of needing to fight everything we see as wrong to simply worshipping God and resting because He fights for us.

Two things will be required of us in this context and Joshua did them perfectly. He offered himself and then obeyed the man's instructions. In this process, he discovered that he was standing on holy ground. Just like that, off came his shoes. Now he was in perfect contact with the holy ground, nothing between the soles of his feet and the path.

Even though we are soldiers for the Lord, let's never forget that we are engaged with Him. The greatest honour will be when He simply says, *"Take off your sandals, for the place where you are standing is holy."*

Day Eighty-Four

ORDINARY PEOPLE HAVE
EXTRAORDINARY ENCOUNTERS

Moses was taking care of the sheep of his father-in-law Jethro, the priest of Midian. As he led the sheep to the far side of the desert, he came to Horeb, the mountain of God.

The Messenger of the Lord appeared to him there as flames of fire coming out of a bush. Moses looked, and although the bush was on fire, it was not burning up. So he thought, "Why isn't this bush burning up? I must go over there and see this strange sight."

When the Lord saw that Moses had come over to see it, God called to him from the bush, "Moses, Moses!"

Moses answered, "Here I am!"

God said, "Don't come any closer! Take off your sandals because this place where you are standing is holy ground. I am the God of your ancestors, the God of Abraham, Isaac, and Jacob." Moses hid his face because he was afraid to look at God. (Exodus 3:1–6, GW)

THESE DYNAMIC ENCOUNTERS God orchestrates are impossible for us to dream of, and even more impossible to actually make happen. But God does it easily.

It had been about forty years since Moses had gone to Median, leaving Egypt and running for his life. Life had gotten into a fairly predictable routine after he married and started working at his job of looking after a flock of sheep. Every day was like the one before, and tomorrow rarely if ever held any promise of change. The sheep depended on him for their lives, and he depended on them for his livelihood. So he took them wherever they needed to go for food. He wasn't looking for God; he was looking for grass for the sheep.

But God had His eye on Moses.

The messenger of the Lord didn't look like anything unusual, until Moses noticed a significant detail: a fire. And not a normal fire! This fire didn't burn up the bush which was supposedly engulfed in flames. That got Moses's attention and disrupted his routine.

He could have just kept going, but he didn't. A life-changing encounter with God was the result. He must have hurriedly taken off his shoes and hid his face. From that day on, his life was never the same.

God has a plan for each of us. Our journeys may seem boring, routine, and without significance, but God has something of importance for us all. Simply take the time to explore the little interruptions on your path. They may introduce you to a completely new encounter with God.

Day Eighty-Five

JUST BE QUIET!

Keep thy foot when thou goest to the house of God,
and be more ready to hear, than to give the sacrifice
of fools: for they consider not that they do evil. Be
not rash with thy mouth, and let not thine heart be
hasty to utter any thing before God: for God is in
heaven, and thou upon earth: therefore let thy words
be few. For a dream cometh through the multitude
of business; and a fool's voice is known by multitude
of words. (Ecclesiastes 5:1–3, KJV)

JOSHUA AND MOSES had two things in common when they encountered God: they both took off their shoes and stopped talking. These
actions are very significant.

In the Hebrew culture, shoes (or sandals) were only worn out-
doors. Most often they were simple and only meant to protect the
sole of the foot. They were always taken off when a person entered
a home, to prevent the wearer from tracking dirt inside. It was also a
statement of respect.

I have lived in northern Canada all my adult life and have gotten
into the habit of taking off my shoes when I go inside. It's customary
here and I do it without even thinking.

However, I become extremely self-conscious when visiting places
where everyone just walks in with their shoes on. I leave mine on as
well and it feels disrespectful, like I'm making everything dirty. Being
so aware of my feet feels weird, but I quickly grow accustomed to it.

Soloman, who was a very wise man, tells us to be aware of our
feet when we enter the house of God. His concern is that we should

know two things about our feet—first, whether they are clean or dirty, and second, that we choose the path on which we place our feet. These things will greatly influence what we do, including how we use our mouths.

We can be sure that when Joshua and Moses discovered they were on holy ground, rushing to take off their shoes, they didn't start rambling on about the difficulties and injustices in their lives. They certainly didn't start promoting themselves. It was quite the opposite! They were silent as they did what they were told. They responded this way because they were clean servants with hearts to follow God.

The fool has no idea of wisdom, honour, or cleanliness. All he has to offer anyone, even God, is lots and lots of empty words. We would all be better off if we would just remember that God is in heaven and we are on earth, so it's best if our words are few!

Day Eighty-Six

TAKE THE LOW PATH

And whoever gives one of these little ones just a cup
of cold water to drink in the name of a disciple, truly
I say to you, he shall by no means lose his reward.
(Matthew 10:42, NASB)

Take heed that ye despise not one of these little
ones; for I say unto you, That in heaven their angels
do always behold the face of my Father which is in
heaven. (Matthew 18:10, KJV)

GOD DOESN'T NECESSARILY choose the greatest people to do His
most significant work. He's not like us.

When I managed an RV dealership, I needed to hire mechanics
to do the repair work. I wanted a qualified person, someone who was
mature, experienced, and trustworthy. After reviewing everyone who
applied for the job, I chose the one who seemed best qualified.

Most of the time, this process worked out. But once in a while
the one who looked like the best actually wasn't. I learned more
about them as we worked together.

One person, after only working a few days, went missing from
the shop during a shift. After paging him several times on the intercom, I finally found him behind the building. I asked what he was
doing and why he hadn't responded to our call.

"Who do you think you are, and why are you telling me what to
do?" he demanded.

Moments later, he was no longer employed.

When God calls us to follow, He doesn't look at our credentials
and then choose the one who appears better than the others. He

looks at our hearts, looking for those who are humble and clean and notice the hungry and thirsty at their doorstep. He looks for the ones who are intent on serving the God of the universe, yet they stop to give a cup of cold water to an insignificant thirsty child. He'll never have to use an intercom or go looking for those with a clean and humble heart, because they'll never be absent. These are the ones who are delighted to be led by the Spirit. This is proven by the fact that they notice the little ones.

In God's kingdom, the rewards don't go to those who serve the biggest meal to the greatest nobleman. They go to the one who does the simplest service for those who cannot pay anything back. God has His eye on the poor and never forgets those who serve them.

> God is fair; he will not forget the work you did and
> the love you showed for him by helping his people.
> And he will remember that you are still helping them.
> (Hebrews 6:10, NCV)

There should never be a question as to who God is or whether He has the right to tell us what to do. We are honoured to serve the King of Kings and blessed when we can give a cup of cold water to a little one.

Day Eighty-Seven
SERVANTS UNAWARE

Then shall the righteous answer him, saying, Lord, when saw we thee an hungred, and fed thee? or thirsty, and gave thee drink? When saw we thee a stranger, and took thee in? or naked, and clothed thee? Or when saw we thee sick, or in prison, and came unto thee? And the King shall answer and say unto them, Verily I say unto you, Inasmuch as ye have done it unto one of the least of these my brethren, ye have done it unto me. (Mathew 25:37–40, KJV)

THERE IS A motivation for everything we do, even though we may not be conscious of it. Eventually, though, we discover what drives us to do the things we do, as well as what drives us not to do things.

One winter I drove into Fort St. John. Just as I got into town, I noticed an old man slowly walking along the road without a hat or gloves, pushing a shopping cart. He was heading out of town, which seemed strange. It was very cold and windy.

But since he was in the opposite lane, I just kept going. I was in a hurry and was sure someone would stop and help him.

As I continued to think about that old man, I grew increasingly uncomfortable. I only travelled a few more blocks before I knew I had to turn around and check on him. He had become more important to me than my own schedule.

I caught up to him and parked the car. We put all his stuff in the back and he got inside, shaking badly from the cold. He was very cold and disoriented, thinking he had been heading into town to buy some gloves. I was honoured to be able to get him warmed up and drop him off at the store.

I'm not sure who that man was. I had never seen him before, and I haven't seen him since. And none of that matters.

Could it be that one small thing we do for a needy person, one who seems to have no place in society, is of greater significance to God than anything else we could do? Big organizations frequently advertise the work they do for God, gathering lots of attention and support. These organizations do good work and impact many people's lives.

But I never want to forget that it's not the great work we consciously do for Jesus that counts. That would make us like the unrighteous ones who were shocked to learn that the work they thought they were doing for Jesus hadn't been done for Him at all.

Those ones with righteous hearts will serve the least ones, the almost unnoticed ones, and not even be aware of who they're serving. The day will come when they'll realize they were actually serving Jesus. The greatest satisfaction is in serving the least.

Day Eighty-Eight

HIS SERVANTS MUST NOT QUARREL!

And the servant of the Lord must not strive; but be gentle unto all men, apt to teach, patient, in meekness instructing those that oppose themselves; if God peradventure will give them repentance to the acknowledging of the truth... (2 Timothy 2:24–25, KJV)

TIMOTHY HAS SOME great instructions for those who delight in being servants of the Lord. This is more than just information about what not to do. These emphatic words, *"must not strive,"* need to be given careful consideration. They must not be minimized and eventually discarded.

Every servant of God who strives eventually becomes ineffective in their service. When we argue, the goal is to overpower and dominate the other with strength. That strength may be based in logic, facts, or simply emotion. But it's contrary to how a servant of God conducts himself.

How should I respond then when I have to deal with the real issues I'm confronted with? Timothy didn't stop at just telling us what not to do. He offered clear instructions that can be difficult to carry out for anyone who has the urge to promote themselves while minimizing others. He said, *"Be gentle unto all men."*

Notice the word *all*. This will require some practice.

With my heart set on serving God, it will be done. When we genuinely have a heart that's gentle and kind, our actions soon reflect it. In the context of arguing, my gentleness would be demonstrated by my ability to use a word rather than a multitude of words. It is simple, gentle, and kind.

> You want things, but you do not have them. So you are ready to kill and are jealous of other people, but you still cannot get what you want. So you argue and fight. You do not get what you want, because you do not ask God. Or when you ask, you do not receive because the reason you ask is wrong. You want things so you can use them for your own pleasures. (James 4:2–3, NCV)

Ask God for the ability to be content using few words. This gives you the ability to be a good teacher. Others grow and learn best in a peaceful environment, in the presence of true servants of God.

Day Eighty-Nine

HUMBLE YOURSELF

> Neither be ye called masters: for one is your Master, even Christ. But he that is greatest among you shall be your servant. And whosoever shall exalt himself shall be abased; and he that shall humble himself shall be exalted. (Matthew 23:10–12, KJV)

ONE OF THE greatest challenges for us is to humble ourselves. To be successful at this, we must have the ability to lower ourselves in every action and attitude.

And yet people have told me that this is impossible to do because it must be a work done by God. It's true that God humbled Israel when He brought them out of Egypt, and he can do so to individuals or nations—but the result will be very different.

A choice that's motivated by my heart has a much greater impact on my life than something that's forced on me. Jesus didn't talk about "whoever gets humbled"; He specifically talked about "he who humbles himself."

The attitude that motivates us to humble ourselves is directly opposite to the one that motivates us to exalt ourselves. If it's possible to exalt myself, it's also possible to humble myself.

Neither of these conditions is permanent. If I lift up myself, I get brought low. And if I bring myself low, I get lifted up. But the reward of getting lifted up, eventually, isn't the motivation that drives us to humble ourselves. The true motivation isn't external. It comes from a condition of the heart; I easily esteem others higher than myself. This kind of living opens the door for great and exciting adventure.

Don't act out of selfish ambition or be conceited. Instead, humbly think of others as being better than yourselves. (Philippians 2:3, GW)

"For everyone who exalts himself will be humbled, and the one who humbles himself will be exalted."

Now He also went on to say to the one who had invited Him, "Whenever you give a luncheon or a dinner, do not invite your friends, your brothers, your relatives, nor wealthy neighbors, otherwise they may also invite you to a meal in return, and that will be your repayment. But whenever you give a banquet, invite people who are poor, who have disabilities, who are limping, and people who are blind; and you will be blessed, since they do not have the means to repay you; for you will be repaid at the resurrection of the righteous." (Luke 14:11–14, NASB)

The blessings of God are like water, flowing downhill. Stay in the lowest place to receive those blessings.

Day Ninety

A SERVANT'S INHERITANCE

No weapon that is formed against thee shall prosper; and every tongue that shall rise against thee in judgment thou shalt condemn. This is the heritage of the servants of the Lord, and their righteousness is of me, saith the Lord. (Isaiah 54:17, KJV)

SERVANTS OF THE Lord have quite an inheritance, especially when you consider the fact that they are servants. The Hebrew people understood very well what a servant was. This was a person who served due to enslavement.

Various Hebrew words for servant are used more than a thousand times in the Old Testament. It was a very common word with a very clear meaning. Servants had no life of their own; it was all about the one they served. Whether the reward for their work was a wage or some living accommodation, it would have been extremely rare to receive any inheritance from their master.

When Jesus called people to follow Him, He made it clear that the follower (also called a disciple) needed to leave everything behind if he was going to successfully serve the Lord. A follower or servant has no anticipation of great riches or a highly elevated position in society. That's not their motivation. Rather, those things drive us to exalt and promote ourselves to attain things that are *"highly esteemed among men"* (Luke 16:15).

I will be compelled to serve Him when I honour Him because I love Him. I can only love Him because He first loved me (1 John 4:19). But honour is different. We receive honour from Him *after* we have given honour to Him. (1 Samuel 2:30)

…and shalt honour him, not doing thine own ways, nor finding thine own pleasure, nor speaking thine own words: then shalt thou delight thyself in the Lord; and I will cause thee to ride upon the high places of the earth, and feed thee with the heritage of Jacob thy father: for the mouth of the Lord hath spoken it. (Isaiah 58:13–14, KJV)

God honours His servants, giving them an amazing heritage. This is better than getting a sum of money dumped in our bank account. It's an inheritance of protection from everything that has been designed to destroy us, including words of accusation and condemnation. The power of these destructive words is nullified by the inheritance given to us as clean servants of God.

Day Ninety-One

FEARFULLY FOLLOWING WITH LITTLE FAITH

And when he was entered into a ship, his disciples followed him. And, behold, there arose a great tempest in the sea, insomuch that the ship was covered with the waves: but he was asleep. And his disciples came to him, and awoke him, saying, Lord, save us: we perish. And he saith unto them, Why are ye fearful, O ye of little faith? Then he arose, and rebuked the winds and the sea; and there was a great calm. But the men marvelled, saying, What manner of man is this, that even the winds and the sea obey him! (Matthew 8:23–27, KJV)

JESUS HAD GREAT patience with His disciples. He knew they didn't have much faith when they followed Him into the boat. He also knew that even though they'd spent lots of time in their boats fishing, they also feared passing through storms on the water.

This particular storm probably stirred up memories. While they franticly bailed out the water, trying to keep the boat from sinking, Jesus slept peacefully. As the disciples watched Him sleep, they could only conclude that He didn't care whether they died.

They wrongly concluded that Jesus didn't care, when actually He was sleeping because He was at peace.

Our conclusions are also wrong when we're in that same condition of being afraid and having only a little faith.

The fact that they were fearful and had only a little faith never disqualified them from being disciples. Jesus clearly told people what was required to follow Him, but He never told people they could only follow Him if they were free from fear and had great faith. This is important because faith and freedom from fear are two things we can never gain on our own. We only get these things from being in His presence over a period of time.

> And he said, Come. And when Peter was come down out of the ship, he walked on the water, to go to Jesus. But when he saw the wind boisterous, he was afraid; and beginning to sink, he cried, saying, Lord, save me. And immediately Jesus stretched forth his hand, and caught him, and said unto him, O thou of little faith, wherefore didst thou doubt? (Matthew 14:29–31, KJV)

Only when I come to Jesus and follow Him do I discover that my faith is small and my fears big. It's impossible to deceive myself when I'm in His presence because His light illuminates every part of my life, changing me.

Jesus's response to Peter shows perfectly how He responds to us when our fear takes control and we begin to sink. Jesus extended His hand to us—and we are changed.

Day Ninety-Two

INTENSE INSTRUCTIONS FOR DISCIPLES

> Then in the audience of all the people he said unto
> his disciples, beware of the scribes, which desire to
> walk in long robes, and love greetings in the mar-
> kets, and the highest seats in the synagogues, and
> the chief rooms at feasts; which devour widows'
> houses, and for a shew make long prayers: the
> same shall receive greater damnation. (Luke 20:45–
> 47, KJV)

JESUS FELT CONCERN for His followers and wanted to instruct them
on how to avoid some of the serious mistakes religious people often make, causing them to try gaining their own followers instead of
themselves being His followers. Those actions are easy to spot when
you're aware of the problem, but they're hard to see if you're right in
the middle of it.

In today's passage, the word *beware* sets a serious atmosphere
for these instructions concerning the scribes. The scribes were those
who, at some point, became responsible for studying and commu-
nicating all the details of the law. Eventually, their superior attitude
led them to believe their interpretation of the law was more important
than the law itself. The admiration they had for themselves drove
them to always appear superior to others. They walked around in
long robes, loved engaging in special greetings in public places, and
expected to be given the highest honours in the synagogues and at
public feasts.

This was bad enough, but Jesus went on to describe more of
their awfulness. The worst of it was that they took advantage of

widows, the most vulnerable women, to profit themselves. Then, to cover up all their awful behaviour, they prayed long religious prayers that were nothing more than empty words.

It's no wonder that, at the end of their lives, all they had coming to them was *"greater damnation."* If they hadn't been so proud, they might have learned the truth about themselves and changed.

> A man's pride shall bring him low: but honour shall uphold the humble in spirit. (Proverbs 29:23, KJV)

Jesus's concern for His disciples back then is the same concern He has for us today—and the instructions are still the same: "Beware. Hold this in your mind. Pay attention to it. Apply it to yourself!" This is intense. We need to pay close attention or we, too, will give up the beautiful, clean, simple life of being a humble servant.

> For I say unto you, That except your righteousness shall exceed the righteousness of the scribes and Pharisees, ye shall in no case enter into the kingdom of heaven. (Matthew 5:20, KJV)

Our love for Jesus gives us a hunger for right living and opens the door to the kingdom of heaven.

Day Ninety-Three

HIS SECURITY FREED HIM TO SERVE

Jesus knew that the Father had given him authority over everything and that he had come from God and would return to God. So he got up from the table, took off his robe, wrapped a towel around his waist, and poured water into a basin. Then he began to wash the disciples' feet, drying them with the towel he had around him.

When Jesus came to Simon Peter, Peter said to him, "Lord, are you going to wash my feet?"

Jesus replied, "You don't understand now what I am doing, but someday you will."

"No," Peter protested, "you will never ever wash my feet!"

Jesus replied, "Unless I wash you, you won't belong to me."

Simon Peter exclaimed, "Then wash my hands and head as well, Lord, not just my feet!" (John 13:3–9, NLT)

JESUS WAS SECURELY anchored in His identity and relationship with God. He knew what He had, where He came from, and where He was going. This wasn't just something He knew in the brain; it was in His heart because of what He had experienced. All that He had heard, seen, and done proved He was the Son of God on His way back to God.

This security gave Him the freedom to comfortably do one of the lowest jobs of a servant: washing people's feet. His work wasn't done out of obligation or pity for people with dirty feet. It was done out of a desire to establish a meaningful connection with His followers.

Jesus did this perfectly, even though it was so radical that Peter declared he would never let Jesus do it to him. But everything changed when Peter learned the valuable connection he would have as a result of Jesus washing his feet.

This work began with the simple action of Jesus getting up from the table while the rest remained seated. He had work to do; the disciples didn't. Jesus was also well aware that servants would get up from a table first while those of greater status stayed seated.

He took off His own outer garment, laid it aside, then got the towel which would be needed to finish the job.

> After washing their feet, he put on his robe again and sat down and asked, "Do you understand what I was doing? You call me 'Teacher' and 'Lord,' and you are right, because that's what I am. And since I, your Lord and Teacher, have washed your feet, you ought to wash each other's feet. I have given you an example to follow. Do as I have done to you. I tell you the truth, slaves are not greater than their master. Nor is the messenger more important than the one who sends the message. Now that you know these things, God will bless you for doing them. (John 13:12–17, NLT)

The greatest teachers are those who show us the truth by example. I was blessed with a dad who was a good example. He showed us what it was like to care for a family. All ten of his children are still blessed today because of him. The greatest compliment I ever receive is when someone says, "You are so much like your dad."

The same is true of the example Jesus left us. He showed us that we can be secure enough in our relationship with God that we lose nothing when we take the lowest place and serve others, expecting nothing in return.

Day Ninety-Four

ACTIONS OF THOSE WHO ADORE HIM

Jesus said to her, "Believe Me, woman, that a time is coming when you will worship the Father neither on this mountain nor in Jerusalem. You Samaritans worship what you do not know; we worship what we do know, because salvation is from the Jews. But a time is coming, and even now has arrived, when the true worshipers will worship the Father in spirit and truth; for such people the Father seeks to be His worshipers. God is spirit, and those who worship Him must worship in spirit and truth." (John 4:21–24, NASB)

WHILE LIVING IN northern British Colombia, I used a dog team in the winter to pull a sled loaded with firewood. In the summer, I couldn't use the sled but I tied packs to their backs so they could carry camping supplies for many miles. They worked hard and were always happy when I put them to work. They were good, strong Alaskan Huskies and very affectionate. They loved working. When I was getting them into their harnesses, they would often lick my hands and look me in the eye. And they'd do the same thing at the end of the day when I took their harnesses off.

Years later, I discovered the real beauty of what those dogs did to me.

What does it look like when a true worshiper actually worships? One thing is certain: this worship is real. It's the action of a clean heart demonstrating its adoration toward Someone who's real.

Words may be involved, but words alone aren't worship. The more we depend on words to show our worship, the less authentic it is. The rules that direct us to perform particular acts that resemble worship most often end up exalting ourselves, taking attention away from God, the only one who's worthy.

> The Lord says: "These people worship me with their mouths, and honor me with their lips, but their hearts are far from me. Their worship is based on nothing but human rules." (Isaiah 29:13, NCV)

There's nothing complex about worship. It's so simple. Those who listened to Jesus talk about true worshipers easily understood what He was saying. When He said that we worship what we know, He wasn't talking about information; He was talking about the reality of something in the heart of the people's culture. There wasn't anything wrong with that, but it couldn't take them any further; if a person wasn't part of the culture, they couldn't worship well.

Jesus opened their eyes to something unheard of. True worshipers aren't directed by rules or customs. They're directed by something as simple and gentle as a breeze from God's presence. The meaning of the word Jesus used for *worship* is defined as "to kiss, like a dog licking his master's hand."[1] These actions might sound weird, but they aren't. They're truthful, sincere, and transparent, motivated by love from a clean heart.

The beauty of true worship will only be known by those ones who have left everything behind to follow Him.

---

[1] "Strong's #4352: Proskuneo," *Bible Tools*. Date of access: August 14, 2024 (https://www.bibletools.org/index.cfm/fuseaction/Lexicon.show/ID/G4352/proskuneo.htm).

Day Ninety-Five

THEN THE OFFERING WILL BE SWEET

Behold, I will send my messenger, and he shall prepare the way before me: and the Lord, whom ye
seek, shall suddenly come to his temple, even the
messenger of the covenant, whom ye delight in: behold, he shall come, saith the Lord of hosts. But who
may abide the day of his coming? and who shall
stand when he appeareth? for he is like a refiner's
fire, and like fullers' soap: and he shall sit as a refiner
and purifier of silver: and he shall purify the sons of
Levi, and purge them as gold and silver, that they
may offer unto the Lord an offering in righteousness.
Then shall the offering of Judah and Jerusalem be
pleasant unto the Lord, as in the days of old, and as
in former years. (Malachi 3:1–4, KJV)

I'VE LEARNED THAT it doesn't take much energy to get dirty. But
what about when you want to get rid of the dirt? A light layer of dust
can be easily brushed away. Deep stains, however, require the attention of strong, costly cleaning products.

A lot of good cleaning products have been taken off the mar-
ket because someone found a tiny amount of something in it that's
deemed hazardous. Even though the product worked really well, we
can't buy it anymore because of this tiny bit of something that may
hurt us.

Malachi stated two very important facts to the children of Israel
about their coming messiah. First, the Lord was definitely coming.
Second, He would do some major cleaning upon His arrival. There

was no question or doubt that He was coming and it would happen very quickly.

But the prospect of a major cleaning raised concern. This cleaning would be about more than just removing some dust. This would be an intense process, making some people want to run from His presence.

Why was it necessary for Him to do this intense cleaning? Specifically, the cleaning was focused on the sons of Levi. The name Levi is understood to refer to being connected or attached. The significance of this was clear: the Lord Himself would be directly involved in the cleaning process of those who were connected to Him.

The same is true for us today.

Unless they're clean, two will be prevented from being bonded together. Whether we're talking about welding metal, gluing wood, or connecting to the Lord, dirt weakens the bonding point.

An intense cleaning must take place, even though it may look like it'll destroy us. We can't let our eyes and hearts get fixed on the process. We must remember that there's a purpose for it. That purpose is for everything we offer Him to be pleasing to Him.

> And we know that all things work together for good to them that love God, to them who are the called according to his purpose. (Romans 8:28, KJV)

> That the trial of your faith, being much more precious than of gold that perisheth, though it be tried with fire, might be found unto praise and honour and glory at the appearing of Jesus Christ... (1 Peter 1:7, KJV)

The greatest delight we can have will come when we know that the Lord is delighted with everything we offer Him, including our clean lives.

I MUST CLOTHE MYSELF PROPERLY

> But now ye also put off all these; anger, wrath, malice, blasphemy, filthy communication out of your mouth... Put on therefore, as the elect of God, holy and beloved, bowels of mercies, kindness, humbleness of mind, meekness, longsuffering... (Colossians 3:8, 12, KJV)

AFTER WORKING ALL day and getting dirty, I always take time to clean up before putting on clean clothes. It's not a hard decision to make. Clean clothes have no effect on dirt, but dirt will certainly affect clean clothes. Even the nicest clean clothes will get dirty. The only solution is to get clean before putting on clean clothes.

The words Paul wrote to the Colossian church instructed them to *"put on"* certain things in their lives. It wasn't like a "thou shalt" command, one that they would be punished for failing to obey. This was more like a description of the normal activities they had done before choosing to follow God. These aren't the sort of actions and attitudes one would choose to "put on" anymore. We were born wearing those clothes, so we aren't responsible for putting them on, but we are responsible for taking them off. Once they're taken off, we can become clean and learn how to clothe ourselves. Then we'll be able to help others get properly clothed as well. This opens the door for true kingdom living.

> For I was an hungred, and ye gave me meat: I was thirsty, and ye gave me drink: I was a stranger, and ye took me in: naked, and ye clothed me: I was sick,

and ye visited me: I was in prison, and ye came unto me. Then shall the righteous answer him, saying, Lord, when saw we thee an hungred, and fed thee? or thirsty, and gave thee drink? When saw we thee a stranger, and took thee in? or naked, and clothed thee? Or when saw we thee sick, or in prison, and came unto thee? And the King shall answer and say unto them, Verily I say unto you, Inasmuch as ye have done it unto one of the least of these my brethren, ye have done it unto me. (Matthew 25:35–40, KJV)

If I have followed the instructions and put on the things that are appropriate for a follower of Jesus, I will instinctively care for the least—the hungry and thirsty prisoners, the naked, the sick, and the strangers who go unnoticed by those who have never learned to clothe themselves with what God wants us to wear. Until I properly clothe myself, I will never be able to clothe others.

If I choose to serve God, following His path and not my own, my actions will be like a shining light that reflects Jesus everywhere I go. The day will come when He says, *"Come, ye blessed of my Father, inherit the kingdom prepared for you..."* (Matthew 25:34)

Day Ninety-Seven

SUCCESSFULLY FORGIVING

Forbearing one another, and forgiving one another, if
any man have a quarrel against any: even as Christ
forgave you, so also do ye. (Colossians 3:13, KJV)

GOD ALWAYS GIVES us a clear picture of everything He expects as
we follow Him. He also points out all the details. There's never any
guesswork involved. God clearly describes how His followers are to
live. He doesn't demand a high level of education or that we learn
to be articulate in our debates, knowing all the details of scripture.

Unfortunately, we sometimes think these things have value. So
we grasp at them and wonder why it's so hard to forgive others when
they offend us.

Paul must have often had to forgive others for what they did to
him. It's clear that he knew the simple process of extending forgiveness to others. Before forgiving one another, he said that people
should forbear one another.

When I forbear others, it means that I hold myself back and put
up with the offences and mistakes of others. This is impossible to do
without a clean heart that enjoys the beauty of living without offence.
When I live this way, it's a clear statement that my life is directed
more by my love for the Lord than it is by love for myself. My love
for Him stimulates love and honour for others, making it possible for
me to put up with every offence. It allows me to easily forgive others.

Therefore I, a prisoner for serving the Lord, beg
you to lead a life worthy of your calling, for you
have been called by God. Always be humble and

gentle. Be patient with each other, making allowance for each other's faults because of your love. Make every effort to keep yourselves united in the Spirit, binding yourselves together with peace. (Ephesians 4:1–3, NLT)

Paul was intense in his instructions to the Ephesians. He didn't write as a great apostle or minister. He simply wrote from the perspective of one who had been captivated by the Lord. It seemed to him to be a noble calling that required him to adjust every aspect of his life. He appropriately reflected the character of the one he served. It wasn't about observing religious rules to make himself look pious. The opposite was true.

We are to always be humble, kind, and patient with each other. These actions of love give us the ability to forbear one another, able to make allowance for each other's faults. No commandment or church doctrine can give you the ability to do this. Only love.

What would our churches be like if we all lived this way?

Day Ninety-Eight

COMPLETING THE JOURNEY

And above all these things put on charity, which is
the bond of perfectness. (Colossians 3:14, KJV)

CAN YOU IMAGINE going on a journey but never being able to complete it? It would be extremely unusual to start a journey and have no destination in mind.

I've travelled many different ways in the north. At times I've walked many miles alone. Sometimes I've been pulled on a sled by a dog team. Other times I've taken a riverboat. I've driven in cars and flown airplanes.

But no matter how I travelled, I could never see the final destination until I got close to it. Significant points along the way alert me to where I am. They can serve as rest stops or places to refuel, but they aren't the goal. You never stop at these places very long.

I once walked a long distance in very cold weather. I prepared as best I could but hadn't known that the temperature would drop to -40°C about an hour before I got home. The cold slowly began to affect me, but I didn't realize it. As it got dark, I became so sleepy that I could hardly walk. All I wanted to do was lay down. I lost every motivation to keep going.

Suddenly I realized that I was heading down a steep drop in the trail. Realizing that I was only one mile from home, I snapped to attention. Everything in me focused on the beauty of my destination. The cold didn't change and the tiredness didn't leave, but knowing my position gave me power over the elements.

I soon made it home, completing my journey.

Our journey as servants following the Lord is similar. At times we feel like we're too tired, cold, and broken to finish. But God always puts something in our path to wake us up and empower us.

Paul instructed the Ephesian church that the Lord had given certain ministries to build up the followers of Jesus, bringing them stability that would take them partway on their journey.

> ...unto the measure [a limited portion] of the stature of the fulness of Christ... (Ephesians 4:13, KJV)

But something greater was needed to propel them the final distance, so they could become everything God had intended for them.

> Instead, as we lovingly speak the truth, we will grow up completely in our relationship to Christ, who is the head. He makes the whole body fit together and unites it through the support of every joint. As each and every part does its job, he makes the body grow so that it builds itself up in love. (Ephesians 4:15–16, GW)

The best, most gifted ministry can never give us what is needed to complete our journey of growth in Christ. All we need is the simple influence of love to propel us across the finish line.

Day Ninety-Nine

THE REIGN OF PEACE

And let the peace of God rule in your hearts, to the
which also ye are called in one body; and be ye
thankful. (Colossians 3:15, KJV)

BEFORE I MET the Lord, anger was my greatest motivator. It was
an ugly way of living. Peace was nowhere to be found. I hurt a lot of
people before my world came crashing in on me.

Thankfully, I found peace with God late one night, setting me on
a different path. I eventually went to bed questioning whether this
peace was real enough to last.

That question was answered the next morning. When I woke up,
I felt a peaceful presence in the room. It was so strong that I didn't
want to move. I made a commitment to God: if this was His peace, I
would follow Him for the rest of my life.

Even though I have gone through some chaotic times since then,
His peace has kept me connected to Him.

> You will keep in perfect peace all who trust in you, all
> whose thoughts are fixed on you! (Isaiah 26:3, NLT)

It's unfortunate that we think we have to struggle and work so
hard, trying to figure out how God wants us to live. We wonder about
what He wants us to do. So we value and trust our own intelligence
and system of religion, so much so that it can be difficult for us to
believe that we can't create peace for ourselves.

This intense struggle makes it impossible for peace to settle in
our lives. This is so different from what Paul had in mind when he
said, *"Let the peace of God rule..."* I can't *make* peace rule; I can

only *let* it rule. This peace will take over and rule my heart after I've heard His invitation to follow and agree to all His conditions. Then I'm no longer my own. I belong to Him and serve Him along with all those others who have heard His call.

As I follow, I begin to understand a bit more of what it's like when peace rules my heart. My eyes are opened and I learn from experience the expectation of His invitation, as well as the eternal greatness of His inheritance.

> The eyes of your understanding being enlightened; that ye may know what is the hope of his calling, and what the riches of the glory of his inheritance in the saints… (Ephesians 1:18, KJV)

> Peace I leave with you, my peace I give unto you: not as the world giveth, give I unto you. Let not your heart be troubled, neither let it be afraid. (John 14:27, KJV)

Jesus gave us peace. If we taste and see how good it is, we'll never let anything else rule our hearts. Trouble and fear will never again distract us on our journeys as we serve Him.

Day One Hundred

HOLD ON, NEVER LET GO

Let the word of Christ dwell in you richly in all wisdom; teaching and admonishing one another in psalms and hymns and spiritual songs, singing with grace in your hearts to the Lord. And whatsoever ye do in word or deed, do all in the name of the Lord Jesus, giving thanks to God and the Father by him. (Colossians 3:16–17, KJV)

WORDS CAN HAVE great power, especially when spoken with authority. However, there's something greater than using many words in a powerful way: using a *single* word, spoken in humility without any drama or attempt to dominate.

This is what the word of Christ is like, singular in its expression of divine authority. If I intend to successfully live as a follower of Jesus, serving Him, the divine expression must have a place of residence in my life. In fact, it must be the only thing that has a place. Then I will have a pure, successful, satisfying life. When I embrace the word of Christ in my heart, it will not only influence my choice of words but also the emotions attached to them.

Thy word have I hid in mine heart, that I might not sin against thee. (Psalm 119:11, KJV)

Let your speech be always with grace, seasoned with salt, that ye may know how ye ought to answer every man. (Colossians 4:6, KJV)

God offers us everything we need to follow Him. Some things I receive from Him are obtained easily, so I just let them have their place in me. Other things aren't automatic. I must take hold of these things.

Paul said it well to Timothy: *"Fight the good fight of faith, lay hold on eternal life, whereunto thou art also called..."* (1 Timothy 6:12, KJV)

At times we'll have to fight, struggling to keep living the lives to which we've been called. This is impossible to do without the grace of God impacting our hearts with His strength. No grace is needed to freely receive the gifts God has given us; we simply receive them and let them influence our lives. But when we give our lives to serve Him, it will take great effort. The only way this can be done is through the power of grace.

> Therefore, brothers and sisters, use more effort to make God's calling and choosing of you secure. If you keep doing this, you will never fall away. Then you will also be given the wealth of entering into the eternal kingdom of our Lord and Savior Jesus Christ. (2 Peter 1:10–11, GW)

When Jesus said, *"Freely ye have received, freely give"* (Matthew 10:8, KJV), He wasn't talking about money or any of the stuff we value. He was talking about *life*.

Receive everything He freely gives you and then serve Him with all your heart, mind, soul, and strength!

ALSO AVAILABLE

ONE OF THE greatest motivators in life is when joy is at the root of your actions, your work will give you great satisfaction. Whether you work as a tradesperson in a shop, or sit in an office, or serve in a church, the joy inside you will set you apart from the rest of the world.

This devotional contains lessons derived from the stories and people written about in the Bible, as well as the real-life experiences of the author. What is your story?